The Émigré Analysts and American Psychoanalysis

This book explores the impact of migration, including its causes, upon the key ideas and directions of psychoanalytic theory and practice from the twentieth century until today.

Having originated with a conference called "Émigré Analysts," developed through the Sandor Ferenczi Center at the New School for Social Research, this collection encompasses a wide array of often personal insights into the historical effects of exile and migration upon psychoanalysis. Divided into three sections, the book first attends to the political crises that affected the exile of psychoanalysts after the Second World War, tracing their journeys from Eastern Europe to the United States; secondly, the rise of antisemitism and the impact of the Holocaust upon these analysts is closely examined; and, finally, this book attends to the protection and safety of analysts forced into exile in our contemporary moment with reference to the work being done by existing national and international psychoanalytic institutions.

As an engaging and thoroughly detailed account of the influence of exile upon American psychoanalysis, this book will be of as much interest to scholars of history and twentieth-century culture as to psychoanalysts and psychoanalytic psychotherapists in training and in practice.

Adrienne E. Harris is faculty and supervisor at the New York University Postdoctoral Program in Psychotherapy and Psychoanalysis. She is on the faculty and is a supervisor at the Psychoanalytic Institute of Northern California. She is an editor of *Psychoanalytic Dialogues* and *Studies in Gender and Sexuality*. In 2009, she, Lewis Aron, and Jeremy Safron established the Sandor Ferenczi Center at the New School University. She and Eyal Rozmarin co-edit the book series Relational Perspectives in Psychoanalysis for Routledge.

RBP

The Relational Perspectives Book Series (RPBS) publishes books that grow out of or contribute to the relational tradition in contemporary psychoanalysis. The term *relational psychoanalysis* was first used by Greenberg and Mitchell[1] to bridge the traditions of interpersonal relations, as developed within interpersonal psychoanalysis and object relations, as developed within contemporary British theory. But, under the seminal work of the late Stephen A. Mitchell, the term *relational psychoanalysis* grew and began to accrue to itself many other influences and developments. Various tributaries – interpersonal psychoanalysis, object relations theory, self-psychology, empirical infancy research, feminism, queer theory, sociocultural studies, and elements of contemporary Freudian and Kleinian thought – flow into this tradition, which understands relational configurations between self and others, both real and fantasied, as the primary subject of psychoanalytic investigation.

We refer to the relational tradition, rather than to a relational school, to highlight that we are identifying a trend – a tendency within contemporary psychoanalysis – not a more formally organized or coherent school or system of beliefs. Our use of the term *relational* signifies a dimension of theory and practice that has become salient across the wide spectrum of contemporary psychoanalysis. Now under the editorial supervision of Adrienne Harris and Eyal Rozmarin, the Relational Perspectives Book Series originated in 1990 under the editorial eye of the late Stephen A. Mitchell. Mitchell was the most prolific and influential of the originators of the relational tradition. Committed to dialogue among psychoanalysts, he abhorred the authoritarianism that dictated adherence to a rigid set of beliefs or technical restrictions. He championed open discussion, comparative and integrative approaches, and promoted new voices across the generations. Mitchell was

"As always, Adrienne Harris brings us to the heart of the intrinsic intertwining of psychoanalysis, politics, and personal history. From its inception in Freud's childhood migration to now, and especially during the rise of Hitler and Nazism, psychoanalysis has been a field of émigrés, immigrants, and refugees. This compelling book, with essays by analysts, historians, and social scientists, portrays this history through multiple lenses: Jewish Vienna and Budapest, women analysts, the impact of McCarthyism, through to the Argentine psychoanalytic diaspora. It reclaims the radical history of analysts and analysis, beautifully balancing history, politics, biography, individual testimony, and resonant accounts of everyday life."

Nancy J. Chodorow *is author of* The Psychoanalytic Ear and the Sociological Eye, Individualizing Gender and Sexuality, The Power of Feelings *and other works*

"This extraordinary book, which comprises several papers by a group of psychoanalysts, offers one of the most thought-provoking insights of a complex and difficult part of the history of psychoanalytical culture and institutions, antisemitism, forced migrations and political activism, and comes as a breath of fresh air in its understanding of the current worldwide political unrest, uncertainty and loss that has ensued. Often complex political and social problems are narrowed down to a very particular narrative which tends to offer slogans and platitudes, but this group of papers written by courageous and insightful psychoanalysts who defy the usual accounts, in which truth becomes an orthodoxy already known to an enlightened few, whose job is to inform everyone else, with ringing statements of condemnation and exhortation. However, this group of papers is based on a broader analytical approach, where truth is a collective discovery, and which reflects on the actual problem and pain confronting individuals in their lives, and the solutions and reliefs which psychoanalysis can offer."

Ronald Doctor *is a fellow of the British Psychoanalytical Society, London, chair of the IPA Psychoanalysis and Law committee, member of the Steering Committee, IPA in the Community and the World, and consultant psychiatrist, West London NHS Trust*

"This book, compiled by Adrienne Harris with chapters by distinguished authors, is a major contribution to the psychoanalytic understanding of migration and loss. The authors address history, theory, and contemporary experiences of migration. They discuss the notions of uprooting and the grief of losing one's place of origin, culture, language, and all that one sees as familiar in day-to-day life. Migration is a bit like losing Mother Earth – it shakes one's identity. But it can also be a source of hope, offering the possibility of enrichment and depth in the encounter with the other and that which is different. To understand the other, the other land, the other society, and one's newly emerging other self, offers the opportunity to walk in the shoes of those that are different from us and develop an ability to understand that which is foreign.

The Émigré Analysts and American Psychoanalysis, edited by Adrienne Harris, is a psychoanalytic effort that challenges us to understand more and discriminate less in a world currently in the grips of prejudice and xenophobia. It includes chapters by distinguished authors from around the world. Among other topics they address the history of the pre-war migration of psychoanalysis from Central Europe to other parts of the world. This diaspora dispersed the seeds of psychoanalysis to grow and develop in distant lands. And in those distant lands, psychoanalysis, like any other immigrant, was enriched in the process. Other authors address theory and related concepts to help us understand what is psychologically involved in the experiences of emigration and exile. It also takes up the very timely topics of political repression and forced migration.

This book is an important contribution to the study of migration. It addresses a topic that has existed since the beginning of humanity. These chapters give us a contemporary vision of the search for new paths that characterize the human race in its inexhaustible desire to discover the unknown, or in its desperate attempts to flee imminent dangers in search of a safe place to survive or even thrive. *The Émigré Analysts and American Psychoanalysis* will enrich your thinking and be a great addition to your library."

Adriana Prengler, *vice president of the International Psychoanalytical Association* later joined by the late Lewis Aron, also a visionary and influential writer, teacher and leading thinker in relational psychoanalysis.

Included in the Relational Perspectives Book Series are authors and works that come from within the relational tradition, those that extend and develop that tradition, and works that critique relational approaches or compare and contrast them with alternative points of view. The series includes our most distinguished senior psychoanalysts, along with younger contributors who bring fresh vision. Our aim is to enable a deepening of relational thinking while reaching across disciplinary and social boundaries to foster an inclusive and international literature.

A full list of titles in this series is available at www.routledge.com/Relational-Perspectives-Book-Series/book-series/LEARPBS.

Note

1 Greenberg, J., and Mitchell, S. (1983). *Object Relations in Psychoanalytic Theory*. Cambridge, MA: Harvard University Press.

The Émigré Analysts and American Psychoanalysis

History and Contemporary Relevance

Edited by Adrienne E. Harris

Routledge
Taylor & Francis Group

LONDON AND NEW YORK

Designed cover image: Nisian Hughes © Getty Images

First published 2023
by Routledge
4 Park Square, Milton Park, Abingdon, Oxon OX14 4RN

and by Routledge
605 Third Avenue, New York, NY 10158

Routledge is an imprint of the Taylor & Francis Group, an informa business

British Library Cataloguing-in-Publication Data
A catalogue record for this book is available from the British Library

Library of Congress Cataloging-in-Publication Data
Names: Harris, Adrienne, editor.
Title: The émigré analysts and American psychoanalysis : history and contemporary relevance / edited by Adrienne E. Harris.
Description: 1 Edition. | New York : Routledge, 2023. | Includes bibliographical references and index.
Identifiers: LCCN 2022056671 (print) | LCCN 2022056672 (ebook) | ISBN 9781032209852 (hardback) | ISBN 9781032209869 (paperback) | ISBN 9781003266228 (ebook)
Subjects: LCSH: Psychoanalysis—United States—History—20th century. | Psychoanalysts—Europe—History—20th century. | Psychoanalysts—United States—History—20th century. | Europe—Emigration and immigration—History—20th century. | United States—Emigration and immigration—History—20th century.
Classification: LCC BF173 .E635 2023 (print) | LCC BF173 (ebook) | DDC 150.19/5—dc23/eng/20230322
LC record available at https://lccn.loc.gov/2022056671
LC ebook record available at https://lccn.loc.gov/2022056672

ISBN: 978-1-032-20985-2 (hbk)
ISBN: 978-1-032-20986-9 (pbk)
ISBN: 978-1-003-26622-8 (ebk)

DOI: 10.4324/9781003266228

Typeset in Times New Roman
by Apex CoVantage, LLC

In memory of Lewis Aron, whose attention to our history inspired this project.

Contents

Selected Bibliography

Aciman, A. (1999). Shadow Cities. In A. Acumen (Ed.), *Letters of Transit, Reflections on Exile, Identity, Language and Loss* (pp. 15–35). New York: New Press.

Adorno, Theodor. (1978). Freudian Theory and Patterns of Fascist Propaganda. In Andrew Arato and Eike Gebhardt (Eds.), *The Frankfurt School Reader* (pp. 118–137). New York: Urizen Books.

Advertisement, International Universities Press. (1945). Box 11, Ernst Kris Papers, Manuscript Division, Library of Congress, Washington, DC.

Akhtar, S. (1999). The Immigrant, the Exile and the Experience of Nostalgia. *Journal of Applied Psychoanalytic Studies* 4:2.

Akhtar, S. (2004). *Immigration and Identity Turmoil, Treatment, and Transformation.* Lanham: Rowman & Littlefield Publ.

Althusser, L. (1971). Ideology and Ideological State Apparatuses (Notes Towards an Investigation). In *Lenin and Philosophy and Other Essays.* New York: Verso.

Aron, L. (1996). *A Meeting of Minds.* Hillsdale, NJ: The Analytic Press.

Bragin, Martha. (2019). Pour a Libation for Us: Restoring the Sense of a Moral Universe to Children Affected by Violence. *Journal of Infant Child and Adolescent Psychotherapy* 18(3).

Breitman, R., and Kraut, A.M. (1987). *American Refugee Policy and European Jewry, 1933–1945.* Bloomington, IN: Indiana University Press.

Butler, J. (1997). *The Psychic Life of Power: Theories of Subjection.* Stanford, CA: Stanford University Press.

Butler, J. (2004). *Precarious Life: The Powers of Mourning and Violence.* Verso: New York.

Cairo, Irene. (2016). The Place Across the Street. In Julia Beltsiou (Ed.), *Immigration in Psychoanalysis, Locating Ourselves.* London and New York: Routledge.

Cooper-White, P. (2018). *Old and Dirty Gods: Religion, Antisemitism, and the Origins of Psychoanalysis.* New York: Routledge.

Chodorow, Nancy. (1989). Seventies Questions for Thirties Women: Gender and Generation in a Study of Early Women Psychoanalysts. Chap. 10 In *Feminism and Psychoanalytic Theory* (pp. 199–218). New Haven and London: Yale University Press.

Damousi, J., and Plotkin, M.B. (Eds.). (2012). *Psychoanalysis and Politics. History of Psychoanalysis Under Conditions of Restricted Political Freedom*. New York: Oxford University Press.

Deleuze, G., and Guattari, F. (1987). *A Thousand Plateaus: Capitalism and Schizophrenia* (B. Massumi, Trans.). Minneapolis: University of Minnesota Press.

Deutsch, Helene. (1973a). *Confrontations with Myself. An Epilogue*. New York: W.W. Norton & Company.

Frank, T. (2009). *Double Exile. Migrations of Jewish-Hungarian Professionals Through Germany to the United States, 1919–1945*. Bern: Peter Lang, European Academic Publishers.

Eissler, K. (1984). Panel: Politics and Analysis in Vienna Before 1938, Part I. Oral History Workshop 21, Archives, American Psychoanalytic Association, Oskar Diethelm Library, Weill Cornell Medical College.

Fanon, F. (2008). *Black Skin, White Masks*. [1957] London: Pluto.

Fermi, L. (1968). *Illustrious Immigrants. The Intellectual Migration from Europe*. Chicago: The University of Chicago Press.

Freidenreich, Harriet Pass. (2002). *Female, Jewish, and Educated. The Lives of Central European University Women*. Bloomington and Indianapolis: Indiana University Press.

Freud, S. (1912). The Dynamics of Transference. *Standard Edition* 12:99–108.

Fromm, E. (1941). *Escape from Freedom*. New York: Avon.

Frosh, S. (2009). Foreignness Is the Quality Which the Jews and One's Own Instincts Have in Common. Anti Semitism, Identity and the Other. In L. Aron and L. Henik (Eds.), *Answering a Question with a Question. Contemporary Psychoanalysis and Jewish Thought* (pp. 345–369). New York: Academic Studies Press.

Glover, E. (1938). Unpublished Letter to Lawrence Kubie. Archives, American Psychoanalytic Association, Oskar Diethelm Library, Weill Cornell Medical College.

Goodwyn, Laurence. (1978). *The Populist Moment*. New York: Oxford University Press, 1978.

Grinberg, L., Grinberg, R., and Festinger, N. (1989). *Psychoanalytic Perspectives on Migration and Exile*. New Haven: Yale University Press.

Harlem, A. (2010). Exile as a Dissociative State. When a Self Is Lost in Transit. *Psychoanalytic Psychology* 27(4):460–474.

Hofstadter, Richard. (1955). *The Age of Reform*. New York, NY: Vintage.

Hollander, N. (1998). Exile, Paradoxes of Loss and Creativity, Brit. *Journal of Psychotherapy* 15:2.

Jacoby, R. (1986). *The Repression of Psychoanalysis: Otto Fenichel and the Political Freudians*. New York: Basic Books.

Jeffrey, W. (1989). After the Anschluss: The Emergency Committee on Relief and Immigration of the American Psychoanalytic Association. *The American Psychoanalyst* 23:2/3.

Kubie, L. (1938). Emergency Committee on Relief and Immigration: Report to the Council on Professional Training and to the General Session of the American

Psychoanalytic Association, Chicago, June 2–3, 1938. *Bulletin of the American Psychoanalytic Association* 1–3:1937–1940.

Kuriloff, E. (2014). *Contemporary Psychoanalysis and the Legacy of The Third Reich. History, Memory, Tradition.* New York: Routledge.

Kuriloff, E. (2022). What Happened to the Baby's Head? Between Victims and Victimizers. *Psychoanalytic Dialogues* 32:505–517.

Mészáros, J. (2010). Progress and Persecution in the Psychoanalytic Heartland: Antisemitism, Communism and the Fate of Hungarian Psychoanalysis. *Psychoanalytic Dialogues*, 20:600–622.

Mészáros, J. (2014). *Ferenczi and Beyond: Exile of the Budapest School and Solidarity in the Psychoanalyic Movement during the Nazi Years.* London: Karnac.

Mészáros, J. (2017). The Saga of Psychoanalysis in Eastern Europe: Repression and Rebirth in Hungary, in Former Czechoslovakia, and Yugoslavia. *História, Ciências, Saúde – Manguinhos*, Rio de Janeiro 24:91–103.

Nunca Más. Informe de la Comisión Nacional sobre la desaparición de personas. Editorial Eudeba, 1984.

Pauley, Bruce. (1992). *From Prejudice to Persecution. A History of Austrian Anti – Semitism.* Chapel Hill, NC: University of North California Press.

Prince, R. (2009). Psychoanalysis Traumatized: The Legacy of the Holocaust. *The American Journal of Psychoanalysis* 69(3):179–194.

Puget, J. (2010). The Subjectivity of Certainty and the Subjectivity of Uncertainty. *Psychoanalytic Dialogues* 20(1):4–20.

Roazen, Paul. (1985). *Helene Deutsch. A Psychoanalyst's Life.* New York: Anchor Press/Doubleday.

Schrecker, E. (2021). *The Lost Promise: American Universities in the 1960s.* Chicago: University of Chicago Press.

Stadler, F., and Weibel, P. (Eds.). (1995). *The Cultural Exodus from Austria.* Vienna, NY: Springer.

Steiner, R. (1989). It Is a New Kind of Diaspora . . . *International Review of Psychoanalysis* 16:35–78. The title is accompanied by this paragraph. "Some notes on the politics of emigration of German and Austrian psychoanalysts during the Nazi persecution based on the correspondence between Anna Freud and Ernest Jones and other documents."

Steiner, R. (2000). *"It Is a New Kind of Diaspora": Explorations in the Sociopolitical and Cultural Context of Psychoanalysis.* London: Karnac Books.

Steiner, R. (2011). In All Questions, My Interest Is Not in the Individual People but in the Analytic Movement as a Whole. It Will Be Hard Enough Here in Europe in the Times to Come to Keep It Going. After All We Are Just a Handful of People Who Really Have That in Mind. . . . *International Journal of Psychoanalysis* 92:505–591.

Szekacs-Weisz, J., and Ward, I. (2004). Lost Childhood and the Language of Exile. London: Imago East West.

Thompson, N.L. (2012). The Transformation of Psychoanalysis in America: The Transformation of Psychoanalysis in America: Émigré Analysts and the New

York Psychoanalytic Society and Institute, 1935–1961. *Journal of the American Psychoanalytic Association* 60:9–44.

Tummala-Narra, P. (2014). Cultural Identity in the Context of Trauma and Immigration from a Psychoanalytic Perspective. *Psychoanalytic Psychology* 31(3):396–409.

Warburg, B. (1948). Summary of the Work of the Emergency Committee on Relief and Immigration of the American Psychoanalytic Association, 1938–1948. Archives, American Psychoanalytic Association, Oskar Diethelm Library, Weill Cornell Medical College.

Zaretsky, Eli. (2004). *Secrets of the Soul: A Social and Cultural History of Psychoanalysis*. New York: Knopf.

Contributors

Adam D. Brown is the vice provost for research and an associate professor of psychology at the New School University, where he directs the Trauma and Global Mental Health Lab. He is also a member of the faculty in the Department of Psychiatry at NYU School of Medicine. His work seeks to understand the mental health impacts of traumatic stress and develop strategies to build capacity for mental health in contexts in which there are significant barriers to care.

Irene Cairo is a training and supervising analyst and faculty member of the Contemporary Freudian Society and a faculty member at the New York Psychoanalytic Society and Institute. Her publications include "The Place Across the Street" in *Immigration in Psychoanalysis, Locating Ourselves*, ed. Julia Beltsiou, Routledge, 2016, and "Babette Interrupted" (in *Finding Unconscious Fantasy in Narrative, Trauma, and Body Pain*, eds. Paula L. Ellman and Nancy R. Goodman, Routledge, 2017). Dr. Cairo was North American chair of the Ethics Committee of the International Psychoanalytic Association (2013–2019) and North American co-chair of the Program Committee for the IPA 52nd Congress (2021). She is in private practice in New York.

The Rev. Pamela Cooper-White is the Christiane Brooks Johnson professor of Psychology and Religion at Union Theological Seminary, New York. She was the 2013–14 Fulbright-Freud Scholar of Psychoanalysis at the Sigmund Freud Museum Vienna and a visiting lecturer at the Universität Wien. She has published ten books, including *Old & Dirty Gods: Religion, Antisemitism, and the Origins of Psychoanalysis*. Her co-edited volume *Sabina Spielrein and the Beginnings of Psychoanalysis: Image, Thought, and Language* (with Felicity Kelcourse) was named a finalist for the National Association for the Advancement of Psychoanalysis

(NAAP) 2020 Gradiva® Award for Best Edited Book. She is currently president of the International Association for Spiritual Care in Switzerland, serves on the Board of the Freud Foundation U.S. (Freud Museum Vienna) and the International Association for Spielrein Studies, and is on the Steering Committee of the Psychology, Culture and Religion Group of the American Academy of Religion. She has lectured frequently across the U.S. and in Vienna, Bern, Budapest, Prague and Jerusalem.

Adrienne E. Harris is faculty and supervisor at the New York University Postdoctoral Program in Psychotherapy and Psychoanalysis. She is on the faculty and is a supervisor at the Psychoanalytic Institute of Northern California. She is an editor at *Psychoanalytic Dialogues* and *Studies in Gender and Sexuality*. In 2009, she, Lewis Aron and Jeremy Safron established the Sandor Ferenczi Center at the New School University. She and Eyal Rozmarin co-edit the book series Relational Perspectives in Psychoanalysis for Routledge.

Emily A. Kuriloff, Psy.D, is a Clinical Psychologist, and a Training and Supervising Analyst at The William Alanson White Institute in New York, where she has just completed an eight year term as the Director of Clinical Education. She is the author of numerous essays and books chapters related to Trauma and its impact on the patient's and analyst's body self, as well as upon all of psychoanalytic theory and praxis. She has recently completed an 8 year term as the Director of Clinical Education at the William Alanson White Institute. Her book, *Contemporary Psychoanalysis and the Legacy of the Third Reich*, (Routledge, 2014) addresses the impact of the Holocaust on seminal thinkers and clinicians, and this the history and traditions of Psychoanalysis.

Judit Mészáros, PhD., Prof. honoris causa, a training and supervising analyst, staff member at the European Psychotherapy Training Institute in Budapest, author or editor of several books, curated exhibitions about *Ferenczi and the Budapest School* (London, Budapest), president of the Ferenczi Society, and psychoanalyst in private practice.at the Freud Museum, London (2004), and the Galeria Centralis of the Open Society Archives, Budapest (2006), and consulted on documentaries on Ferenczi's life (2001, 2012). She was one of the authors (together with Carlo Bonomi) of the Ferenczi House Project (2006–2011) finished by purchasing the former office of Ferenczi's original villa in Budapest. Now it serves as the Ferenczi Center and Archives. She is the president of the Ferenczi Society, a Board Member of the International Sándor Ferenczi Network, as well as a psychoanalyst in private practice.

Klara Naszkowska is a Polish Jewish research scholar, educator, writer, and organizer. She is a recipient of a Fulbright Fellowship at Union Theological Seminary in New York and the Founding Director of the International Association for Spielrein Studies. Naszkowska is a cultural historian of Jewish East–Central and Eastern European women, working in the fields of gender and women's history, and emigration studies. She is currently completing her research on the diaspora of Jewish East–Central and Eastern European female mental–health professionals in the U.S. (1880–1940), writing a narrative nonfiction book, *Clara Happel, Judaism, and Psychoanalysis in America: Memory, History, and Interpretation* (Routledge Press, 2024), and editing a book on the foremothers of psychoanalysis (Routledge Press, 2023).

Kendall A. Pfeffer is a third-year clinical psychology PhD student at The New School. Her research is focused on mental health capacity-building, with a focus on developing and adapting training and supervision methods for task-sharing interventions delivered in community settings. She received her master's in mental health counseling at the University of Houston and master's in psychology at the New School.

Ellen Schrecker is a historian who has written extensively about McCarthyism and higher education. Her books include *No Ivory Tower: McCarthyism and the Universities*, *Many Are the Crimes: McCarthyism in America* and, most recently, *The Lost Promise: Universities in the 1960s*.

Rogelio A. Sosnik is a training and supervising analyst with the Buenos Aires Psychoanalytic Association, and a training, supervising, and faculty member at the Contemporary Freudian Society (U.S.). He is also member of The American Psychoanalytic Association and the IPA. He is a board member of the *International Journal of Psychoanalysis*. He has published numerous papers in the U.S., Argentina, Uruguay and Italy. He is member of the IPA Committee on Emigration and Relocation and is in private practice in New York City.

David Srivastava is a trained emergency and internal medicine physician. He has worked in primary to tertiary care in many countries, including remote areas and naval medicine. He is a lecturer at the University of Bern and his research focuses on vulnerable populations in the emergency department and staff resilience.

Julia Superka is a third-year PhD candidate in clinical psychology at The New School for Social Research. Her research is focused on understanding the impact of traumatic stress on autobiographical memory, self-identity and future thinking. She received her master's in psychology at The New School.

Nellie L. Thompson is an historian and member of the New York Psychoanalytic Society and Institute, where she serves as the curator of the Brill Library's Archives and Special Collections. She chairs the APsaA Committee on History, Archives and Library; the IPA History of Psychoanalysis Committee; and is a member of the Board of the Sigmund Freud Archives. Her current research interests include the writings of mid-twentieth century psychoanalysts and the role of women early in the psychoanalytic movement.

Eli Zaretsky is a professor of history at the New School for Social Research. He is the child of immigrants; a native of Brooklyn, New York; has a background in the New Left, the civil rights movement and socialist feminism; and has published widely on the history of psychoanalysis. He is a founding editor of *Socialist Revolution*. His works include *Capitalism, the Family and Personal Life*; *Secrets of the Soul: A Social and Cultural History of Psychoanalysis*, *Political Freud*; and "My Life and Psychoanalysis" in *American Imago*, 2016. All these works, except for the last, revolve around the relationship of capitalism, the family and human psychology. He is also the editor of *The Polish Peasant in Europe and America*, a classic study of immigration. His chapter is based on his current research, tentatively entitled "The Mass Psychology of Liberalism," a work inspired by the question of what liberalism might look like if it were based on the idea of the unconscious, rather than on Hobbesian self-preservation and Homo economicus alone.

Introduction

Adrienne E. Harris

My interest in the intersect of the history of psychoanalysis and the history of radical thought and action in American political and cultural history is longstanding. My involvement and attention to political life, history and activism was formed in the 1960s when I was in graduate school at the University of Michigan, a campus very much radicalized by the formation and presence of SDS (Students for a Democratic Society). Retrospectively, I came to understand that the degree and scope of on-campus activism in that era had something to do with the context and background of activism in the American Midwest. A campus like Michigan was profoundly influenced by the labor movements and civil rights activities around Detroit from the 1930s onward. It turns out, as with so many movements and events, that the run-up and pre-history is often more extensive and potent than we imagine. I think the essays and projects reported in this book make that clear. I can see now that this book of essays and the conference where these discussions were set out is about reclaiming our history: our radical history and our trauma history.

When I became more involved with psychoanalysis, in the context of the NYU Postdoctoral Program in Psychoanalysis and Psychotherapy, that institution's history and what I learned over a long friendship with Lewis Aron, my interest in the political and cultural surround of our discipline only deepened. At my institute and in dialogue with friends like Lew, I learned to think about the intersect, the intrusions and exploitation of the clinical worlds, and theories by the social and political surrounds. In 2012, when Lewis Aron, Jeremy Safran and I opened the Sandor Ferenczi Center, history and contemporary possibilities for both studying our history and making new inroads in psychoanalysis, politics and history seemed deeply possible and very exciting.

DOI: 10.4324/9781003266228-1

As the planning and preparation for the conference on this topic evolved at the Sandor Ferenczi Center at the New School, I could feel a variety of complex, often contradictory emotions. I realized I had been wanting to do such a meeting for a long time. Yet, at the moment the conference took place on December 13 and 14, 2019, I realized that while I was undertaking this project with many colleagues I admire and count on as witnesses and commentators on the wider issues of migration and exile in the context of the Second World war, I was also mindful of the absence of colleagues and partners whose view of these issues has been formative for my own.

This book of edited essays emerged from a conference on Émigré Analysts held at the Sandor Ferenczi Center in mid-December (Dec. 13 and 14) in 2019, nine months after Lew Aron's death from cancer in March of that year. His spirit is present in so much of what the Ferenczi Center does and stands for, but, for me, is very much present in this project. Lew's work on our psychoanalytic history shifted so much ground in psychoanalysis and, for me, this work was a seminal project in the larger task of making our histories in psychoanalysis and social and political culture sensible and available to our and upcoming generations.

By the time this conference was planned and took place in 2019, interesting changes were occurring in many different sites and cultures. The conference thus addressed our psychoanalytic history, the American situation in the postwar period and the potent effects of McCarthyism – a time of draconian political repression and surveillance. Also covered were the current circumstances of political unrest and agitation and the forced migrations that ensued. During the conference, and this was my dream, we were able to look at the history of psychoanalytic culture and institutions, philosophy, movements of liberation and antisemitism, and political activism woven into an emerging understanding of a complex difficult part of our history, including McCarthyism.

I think it is probably appropriate that I write this introduction with a mixture of determination and melancholy. There are many lost voices in psychoanalysis in the period of the prewar and wartime of the 1930s and 1940s. But I am also mindful of the contemporary lost voices who taught me and many of us so much about how history shapes and contours a discipline. Bob Sklar, Lew Aron, Jeremy Safran and Muriel Dimen are particularly in my mind as I work on this introduction.

Organization

This book has three sections, allowing the reader to examine the history of prewar migration in psychoanalysis, providing theoretical tools to think about migration and exile and the underlying values in our work, and finally to consider the contemporary experiences of migration and political repression. To only address the past and history, in the context of our current moment, would have been unthinkable. I wrote this introduction and then the pandemic arrived. To be launching this book now, over two years into a worldwide catastrophe that has altered virtually every aspect of social, political, professional and natural life is, I believe, fortuitous. We see here how an earlier generation coped with catastrophe, how upheaval and profound and unexpected change is deeply traumatic AND offers opportunities for transformations and growth at many levels. We offer this book and its record of challenge and determination as a record of our history and as a hope for our future.

Section 1 Émigré Stories and the Political Context

This section is attentive to both the American stories of migration and that political context, the European background and the practical implications and changes that evolved. Nellie Thompson's essay brings together a number of strands in the emigre analysts' experiences, both in the flight from Europe and in the impact on the discipline, the documentation and writing, and the practice of psychoanalysis in the United States. Ellen Schrecker brings an interdisciplinary attention to the political, intellectual and social background that the rise of McCarthyism and political repressions brought on. Flight may have been lifesaving, but the task of integrating into a world, both conservative and often antisemitic, was certainly challenging.

In two chapters by European analysts, we can see the context for flight and the challenge to the continuation of psychoanalysis in central Europe. Judith Meszaros characterizes the situation in Hungary as "two forced exiles" happening within a time of less than two decades, with exile within Europe and exile to North America. The costs and anguish of these changes tell a dark story. One complex strand of this story, which Klara Naszkowska attends to, is the fate of the idealisms, hopes, friendships, and the social and political commitment of that interwar period in Europe. Utilizing long-forgotten personal-history materials and original interviews, she charts the continuities and dimensions of five women psychoanalysts who were close friends in Vienna and the challenges to professional and personal health and optimism in the face of very dire struggles.

Emily Kuriloff's chapter builds on her important and groundbreaking work on the experience of European psychoanalysts in both flight from the danger of fascism in Europe and the complexity of creating new lives and practices in the complex political and professional structures of North America. There is a great deal of pain in these stories and, what is painful but necessary for North American psychoanalysis to really absorb and reflect on, is that there is the still-necessary task of American accountability for the difficulties and failures of this project. This collection is, for me, one commitment (we will need others) to keep our attention on this moment in our history, its tragedies and its powers.

Part 11: Philosophy and Social Context

Pamela Cooper-White's essay is about antisemitism and its role in the origins of psychoanalysis. Her research points to the significance of the position of the first analysts as Jews on the margins of Viennese society as formative of a theory that would analyze *from the underside* what lay beneath every surface of the human psyche. Freud's focus and fascination with classical artifacts is well-known and well-documented. His linking of psychoanalytic method and archeology is well-known, but here Cooper-White notes the avoidance of the real and present dangers of the political scene evolving in the twentieth century with his focus on ancient artifacts. She concludes with a call for contemporary analysts to be attentive to parallel social and political dangers in our own time.

Eli Zaretsky's chapter tracks the not-well-enough-known history of psychology of the group, or mass psychology, as it evolved in Freud's thinking. This chapter fills in the details of as aspect of Freud's work, not so usually in view, but crucial for this project. Zaretsky notes the contemporary relevance of this work as well as its historical roots. It is, as he suggests, the story of irrational forces in history – a story both of the past and deeply important in our current circumstances. In his chapter, Zaretsky tracks the evolution of mass psychology in the Kleinian and Lacanian perspectives, but focuses his attention on the historical roots of these developments: the Frankfort school of critical theory (Fromm, Adorno and Marcuse).

Part 111: Contemporary Contexts

Irene Cairo's chapter, The Exile Within, focuses on memory, memories, forgetting and remembering for that special category of migrant: the exile. She makes the important analysis that, for the exile, when there is no possibility of return, there is a conscious effort and perhaps always also an unconscious need to suppress, ignore or "delete" memories. Such a process, of course, can never be totally successful. Inevitably, this process is fragile. Cairo makes the interesting and important argument that the cost of repression extends beyond just the content of the subject's experience of loss in exile and migration. The mind and heart are overall compromised and wounded.

Rogelio Sosnik's contribution considers Psychoanalysis Emigration and Relocation Com (PERC), which was created in 2017. His essay takes up two primary factors that deeply effect contemporary psychoanalysis in a wide variety of geographic and political settings. We are in a circumstance globally and locally where walls, camps, and the separation and destruction of families and domestic units creates a new level of terror and danger. In this chapter, Sosnik argues that we need a psychoanalytic theory to give an account of the impact of these new forms of terrorism and social control over individuals.

The final essay in this collection comes from Adam Brown and his colleagues, who are doing serious investigative work on the plight and situation of contemporary immigrants, particularly children who are in considerable danger. While most of this collection has focused on migration over the earlier years of psychoanalysis and the earlier years of the twentieth century, we include this chapter by Brown and colleagues to make clear the abiding and dangerous presence of migration both as necessity and as dangerous challenge.

Why has this project been so important to me? I think of a paper Nancy Chodorow wrote, "Children Born Into a World At War." She and I, and our peers, were born in and into the shadow of the second World War, with the immediate experiences of fathers in the army, disruption and the terrible unfolding of the Holocaust as that news made its way into North American consciousness. My father enlisted in the Canadian Army in 1939 and in 1941; four months before I was born, he shipped out. I meet him for the first time in the fall of 1945.

My first serious therapist was Hungarian. I am sure a line stretches to Ferenczi somehow and somewhere. She had emigrated to the Midwest, but it was only decades later when I began to understand the history of migration and exile for psychoanalysts that I understood this trajectory might not have been entirely of her own choosing.

This topic, I understand more and more clearly, has been part of an unconscious and conscious project to deconstruct my own history as well as to make a contribution to our collective history of war and exile and recoveries, as psychoanalysts and citizens.

Part 1

Chapter 1

Émigré Analysts and the Transformation of Psychoanalysis in America

Nellie L. Thompson

My remarks this morning will briefly address three interconnected topics related to the immigration of European psychoanalysts to America. First, the activities undertaken by the Emergency Committee on Relief and Immigration (ECRI) in facilitating the immigration of émigré analysts. Second, the transformative impact of émigré analysts on the New York Psychoanalytic Society and Institute. And third, the creation in 1945 of *The Psychoanalytic Study of the Child* by émigré analysts.[1]

The Emergency Committee on Relief and Immigration (ECRI)

In December 1937, the increasingly complicated situation surrounding the migration of European analysts to the United States led the American Psychoanalytic Association's (APSA) Counsel on Professional Training to form a Committee on the Relations of APSA to the IPA. Its mandate was to study and "deal with all problems arising in connection with the migration of analysts from Europe to this country" (Kubie, 1938a, p. 65). Several problems confronted the committee. First, European analysts were coming to the United States in an ad hoc manner. In some cases, individuals were sponsored by friends or family members, while in other instances analysts were sponsored by a psychoanalytic society. The committee wanted to have a clearer idea of who was coming, where they were settling and the nature of their qualifications. The latter question is directly related to the second problem before the committee. That is, the International Psychoanalytical Association (IPA) had reserved for itself the right to appoint instructors or training analysts. This development greatly agitated American psychoanalysts who feared they were going to be presented with émigré analysts who had been given the seal of approval as instructors or training analyst by the IPA, but whose qualifications they had not vetted.

DOI: 10.4324/9781003266228-3

A few months later, however, in March 1938, the *Anschluss* in Austria drastically changed and complicated the environment for analysts wishing to emigrate and for those in America wishing to aid them. In response to this worsening and dangerous situation, the American Psychoanalytic Association on Sunday, March 13, created the Emergency Committee on Relief and Immigration. Initially its mandate was to facilitate the emigration of Austrian analysts to the United States, but this was soon expanded to include all European analysts and indeed any individual who sought the committee's assistance. No litmus test was applied in determining which individuals would be helped; the committee made every effort to assist anyone who contacted them.

Lawrence Kubie, the secretary of APSA, was appointed Chair of the Emergency Committee. His indefatigable energy and sense of purpose were well-suited to this task. Kubie was very ably assisted by Bettina Warburg, who was appointed co-chair in July of 1938, and Bertram Lewin was named treasurer; all were members of the New York Psychoanalytic Society (NYPS). The Committee's myriad activities can be traced in the detailed information bulletins that first Kubie and then Bettina Warburg wrote to the membership of the American Psychoanalytic Association. Letters written by Kubie to Franz Alexander, President of APSA, and Ernst Jones and Edward Glover in England, also vividly and poignantly convey the pressures and sometimes intractable problems that confronted Kubie, Warburg and their committee, which was composed of members from the Boston, Washington, Baltimore and Chicago societies, as they sought to rescue their colleagues in Europe. For example, the desperate sense of urgency that accompanied the work of the Emergency Committee and the obstacles it confronted are illustrated in a report written by Kubie on March 19, six days after the committee was formed. He reported that "trustworthy information" was now available on the situation in Austria. Ruth Mack Brunswick had telephoned him early that morning immediately after her arrival in Paris from Vienna, and he had been in contact with officials in the State Department. Kubie wrote:

> The information from Austria indicates the seriousness of the local situation in Vienna, with carefully organized confiscation of property, minute searching of private homes, although today none of "our friends" have been physically harmed, although some money was seized from the Verlag. Efforts are being made to persuade Freud to leave and Ernst Jones

is in Vienna . . . at present no Jew is allowed to leave Austria under any circumstances nor is it settled what form of passport or travelling permit will be issued, to replace the former Austrian passport . . . it is highly unlikely that anyone will be allowed to emigrate for several weeks . . . this gives the Committee some time to take more deliberate action. The State Department is anxious to avoid any action that will hurt anyone in Austria. Their view is that anyone the regime wants to seize they will since they came to power with lists of wanted people and then systematically took them into custody. . . . With more planning, there is less danger that people will be turned back at the border or having their papers confiscated.

(Kubie, 1938a)

Two weeks later, on March 31, Kubie circulated an ominous report concerning the situation in Austria, writing that it was, "If anything, more distressing than before." Only a few individuals had been allowed to leave Austria and the emigration of Austrian Jews was a rare occurrence. When they were allowed to leave, they could only take 20 Austrian shillings (about $4.00), so they were utterly destitute when they crossed the border. Kubie reported that the Committee had managed to secure affidavits for a large number of analytic colleagues in Austria, so that when the ban on emigration was lifted, those who were not going on to other European countries would at least have the opportunity to secure an American visa. He pleaded for more donations:

   Money must be poured into Dr. Lewin's fund at once . . . this money [is] to be used for food, shelter, traveling expenses for those who reach these shores . . . and their living expenses starting the first month after their arrival. It is immediately and urgently essential that we contribute anything that we possibly can as individuals, and at the same time for every one of us to appeal to every available friend for donations, both large and small. Please send money at once to Dr. Bertram Lewin.

(Kubie, 1938b)

Letter to Ernst Jones, April 26, 1938

On April 26, Kubie wrote to Ernst Jones to express the Committee's wish that he communicate the following to colleagues who wish to come to America. They should be made aware of the fact that the larger cities already have well-organized societies and institutes and are well-equipped with training analysts. On the other hand, there are many cities where there is a need for psychoanalysts, and refugees will be encouraged to settle in those cities and areas of the country. Kubie acknowledges, however, that this will be difficult for many colleagues from Europe. Each prospective immigrant will be asked by the Committee to complete a questionnaire with full data on their training. Each individual will also be provided with an **Information Bulletin** (Appendix A) in order to give he or she a full picture of the situation they will meet when they come to America (Kubie unpublished letter to Ernst Jones, 1938c).

The **Information Bulletin** is a daunting document describing in great detail the situation in the United States the émigrés will confront regarding licensing and the practice of psychoanalysis. It was a rather chilling document to read for analysts trapped in Europe and fearing their lives were in danger. Kubie felt many émigrés misunderstood the **Information Bulletin** and was frustrated by their belief that APSA was responsible for the tangle of state laws governing the practice of medicine and psychoanalysis, as well as for the impasse over the status and fate of lay analysts who emigrated to America. Kubie was frustrated as well by what he called this "ridiculous panic" among American analysts concerning the emigration of European analysts to the United States voiced by their fear that they would lose patients to the newly arrived European analysts.

One element overlooked when this "panic" is cited is the fact that in 1938, APSA was a small organization that was created from a federation of four societies: Boston, Chicago, New York and Washington. It had a membership of 140 analysts, of whom 18 were émigrés. The largest society was the NYPS, with 72 members. By 1939, two more societies, Philadelphia and Topeka, had joined the APSA, boosting its membership to 183, including **29** émigrés. The fact that the APSA was a relatively small organization makes the success of the Emergency Committee in facilitating the immigration and resettlement of émigré analysts, including many lay analysts, an impressive achievement. However, the vexed issue of how to treat lay analysts would haunt APSA for decades and cast a shadow over the work of the Emergency Committee.

Yet the "panic" induced by the arrival of émigré analysts seems to have quickly dissipated as soon as they became members of existing psychoanalytic societies. This was certainly the case with the NYPS. In 1937, the society had 71 members, of whom five were émigrés, and was the largest psychoanalytic society in the United States (IPA Bulletin, IJP, 1937). A decade later, in 1948, its membership was 152, with 51 – a full third – being émigrés. Half of these émigrés were originally members of the Vienna Psychoanalytic Society, and this probably accounts for the fact that the émigré members of the NYPS are often referred to as "The Viennese." To do so, however, is misleading, as ten émigré members formerly belonged to the Hungarian Psychoanalytic Society, among them Robert Bak, Margaret Mahler and George Gerõ, a lay analyst who was a Special Member of NYPS. He had a close relationship with Otto Fenichel and was part of the circle of analysts who received Fenichel's Rundbriefe. The Berlin Psychoanalytic Society was represented by 9 members, among them Edith Jacobson, Henry Lowenfeld and Edward Kronold. The last figure is not very well-known outside of NYPS, but Kronold played an important role in the society and was an original member of the Sigmund Freud Archives. Thus, the psychoanalytic cultures of the three leading European psychoanalytic centers – Berlin, Budapest and Vienna – all made their influence felt within the NYPS. In 1961, when the society observed its 50th anniversary, all the of the officers of the institute were émigrés (president, Annie Reich; vice-president, Annemarie Weil; secretary, Nicholas Young; treasurer, Dora Hartmann), as was the chair of the Educational Committee (Robert Bak). Nine of the 17 members of the EC were émigré analysts: Heinz Hartmann, Edith Jacobson, Edward Kronold, Rudolph Loewenstein, Margaret Mahler, Annie Reich and Nicholas Young, and the register of 57 training analysts included 25 émigrés.

ECRI's Final Report by Bettina Warburg

On May 10, 1943, at the APSA spring meeting, the Emergency Committee reported that "its work had come to a conclusion as no further immigration from Europe was possible and all the individuals who had reached the United States were established in various parts of the country." In 1948, Bettina Warburg wrote a 45-page summary report of the Emergency Committee's work (1938–1948) that included information on 254 individuals with whom the Emergency Committee had been in contact, descriptions of the assistance rendered them and individuals it had been unable to assist (Warburg, 1948).

Individuals were grouped according to the nature of their contact and the assistance rendered them. There were four groups: persons in the U.S. assisted financially (51), persons outside the U.S. assisted financially (41), persons in the U.S. in contact with the committee (134) and persons who requested affidavits (55). Of the 254 individuals the Emergency Committee assisted, 99 were psychoanalysts, lay analysts or candidates who completed their training in the United States. This group included, among others, Otto Fenichel, Annie Reich, Heinz Hartmann, George Gerõ, Theodor Reik and Robert Bak. While the emphasis is often on the number of psycho-analysts rescued by the committee, the fact should not be forgotten that it also assisted a diverse, larger group of individuals: psychologists, social workers, nursery school teachers, non-analytic physicians, including psy-chiatrists, and family members of analysts. Warburg's account also detailed the challenging, and sometimes intractable, difficulties encountered in the effort to obtain visas for individuals seeking to flee Europe. Before a visa could be granted, the applicant had to demonstrate that they could pay for their passage and have an affidavit signed by a sponsor who guaranteed, if needed, financial support for the émigré. Given the bureaucratic and finan-cial obstacles encountered in securing the emigration of individuals who sought ECRI's assistance, the Committee's achievement in assisting so many individuals who sought their assistance was remarkable.

Warburg's 1976 Report

In 1976 the Research Foundation for Jewish Immigration asked Bettina Warburg to write a report on the work of ECRI. In her report, Warburg made the striking observation that while many émigrés experienced pro-found feelings of dislocation after arriving in the United States, they were often reconciled to their new environment by geography.

> An interesting finding from the psychoanalytic point of view, was the importance of the landscape and the need to establish a home resem-bling that of the native country as closely as possible. Individuals readily accepted locations in faraway places given that they were provided with the desired mountains and seascapes.
>
> (Warburg, 1976)

Upon reading this, it suddenly occurred to me that the NYPS is located in Yorkville, a neighborhood on the Upper East Side that was settled by German and Hungarian immigrants in the early 20th century. While Yorkville lacked "mountains and seascapes," it did have shops and restaurants – a German bakery, deli and marzipan shop; Hungarian restaurants, a bookstore and a church – that provided émigré members a familiar environment as they adjusted to their new lives. Importantly, Yorkville was a neighborhood whose fabric was interwoven with the German and Hungarian language.

Among the themes that occur in recollections of émigrés relating to their forced exile and their feelings about their new home, two are notable. One is that their feelings of dislocation were concentrated around the necessity of having to learn a new language, including its slang and vernacular expressions, while simultaneously navigating the challenge of doing clinical work in English. Émigré analysts identified with a European cultural milieu that valued verbal fluency and took pleasure in speech and conversation. Peter Neubauer has described how difficult it was to step into a new language.

I felt unable to communicate, and when you come from Vienna, to speak and to articulate, and to talk, is something which is not only expected but which you very much enjoy doing. And to find yourself limited in your ability to articulate and to express yourself, was for the first, year and a half, for me an extraordinarily difficult one.

(Neubauer, 1986, p. 20)

Helene Deutsch, in a 1942 letter to Raymond Gosselin, the editor of *The Psychoanalytic Quarterly*, voiced the difficulties she was encountering in thinking and writing in two languages.[2]

[A] manuscript of mine is still with the editors of the Quarterly. You are kind enough to speak of my "brilliant writings", but I myself have the feeling that since I am trying to think and write in two languages at the same time, my publications are much worse than before. I would ask you, therefore, to have the publication which is now in your hands, (Emotional Disturbances – Schizophrenia) corrected very thoroughly. Maybe you know of someone who would do it for me for a suitable payment. The difficulties of language and the discontent with my English form is also the reason why I have not sent you yet my manuscript about "Psychoanalytic Therapy". But I have decided to go back to thinking in German and then to have the work translated by a good translator.

With the very best regards,

Sincerely yours, Helene Deutsch

The second theme found in the recollections of many émigré analysts, among them, Margaret Mahler, Peter Neubauer and Ernst Kris, is that coming to America afforded them professional opportunities and experiences that most likely would have been closed off to them in Europe. Margaret Mahler, for example, was quite open about the fact that she felt that professionally she had opportunities here that she would not have had in Europe. Peter Neubauer eloquently spoke about his experiences in America:

> What happened here professionally had such an extraordinary impact on us, there was the development of child psychiatry, there was the development in the way of child analysis, there was development of the analytic applications into many fields, there was the beginning of infant psychiatry, there was the child guidance movement, there was an impact of momentum of building over those last years, which was absolutely encompassing and engaging, and it had a strong influence on the possibilities one could carry out here, while in Europe during the same period was far behind.
>
> (Neubauer, 1986, p. 29)

When Ernst Kris arrived in New York he had already enjoyed a distinguished career as an art historian and psychoanalyst. Once here, his work as a psychoanalyst took on dimensions that embraced a myriad of new activities, including accepting Milton Senn's invitation in 1948 to conduct longitudinal research studies of young children at the Yale Child Study Center, a collaborative endeavor that included pediatricians, nursery school teachers and social workers. This remarkable opportunity afforded Kris the opportunity to study the artistic activity of young children during their years in nursery school. In the papers that followed, Kris recorded his observations on the evolution of the child's use of paint and color, their unruly unconscious fantasies, conflicts and impulses, and the factors that enabled young children to achieve greater control over their creative process (Thompson, 2014).

An Émigré Response to Dislocation, Trauma and Loss: the Psychoanalytic Study of the Child

In 1945, an advertisement which was distributed by the publisher described a new journal, the *Psychoanalytic Study of the Child* (PSOC), edited by Anna Freud, Ernst Kris and Heinz Hartmann. It gave voice to psychoanalysis as a body of knowledge that could enable adults to mediate between the child and the precarious postwar world:

> The future of our society will depend on the capacity of our children to withstand the ever-mounting tensions in the world of today and tomorrow. To guide the formative years of this generation is the critical task facing those who have assumed this responsibility. Adequately to do this requires both a genuine understanding of the mental and psychic development of the child, as gained through psychoanalysis, and the knowledge of how to translate these insights into practice. *The Psychoanalytic Study of the Child* will appear yearly and will therefore, be a permanent guide for experts and specialists in the field of child study. Social workers, teachers, psychiatrists, pediatricians, sociologists and anthropologists will find it an indispensable source of up-to-date information.

This statement of purpose articulated modern aims, still valid today, that were originally outlined at the editorial board's meeting on July 11, 1944. In attendance were Phyllis Greenacre, Heinz Hartmann, Ernst Kris, Lawrence S. Kubie, Bertram Lewin and Marion G. Putnam. Absent from the meeting were Otto Fenichel, Anna Freud, Edith B. Jackson, Rene Spitz, Edward Glover and Willi Hoffer. The *PSOC* was envisioned as an Anglo-American endeavor, and Edward Glover and Willi Hoffer, along with Anna Freud, represented Great Britain. The journal would fulfill its mission by seeking contributions in the following areas: theoretical contributions to the genetic, or developmental, aspects of psychoanalysis; direct observations of children in therapy and outside the consulting room, in guidance clinics, schools and observational and therapeutic nurseries; and reconstruction from adult analysis of typologies of childhood development. These aims encapsulate the roles that analysts envisioned for psychoanalysis and themselves in an uncertain postwar world.

The immediate postwar years were a time of mourning for many émigré analysts as they contemplated their immediate past and their uncertain future, and one may view the establishment of *The Psychoanalytic Study of the Child* as a creative response to the dislocation and losses they had recently endured. It fulfilled a crucial need for many psychoanalysts in the aftermath of the dissolution of the European psychoanalytic community, the geographic dispersal of its members, the Controversial Discussions in the British Society and Anna Freud's decision in 1947 to establish the

Hampstead Child Therapy Training Course outside the confines of the British Society, which in 1952 was followed by the Hampstead Child Therapy Clinic.

For émigré analysts in the United States and London, and like-minded British and American colleagues, *The Psychoanalytic Study of the Child* was a venue in which they continued to consider and develop Freud's last revisionary psychoanalytic contributions. The journal's creation represented an act of restitution and an effort to recreate a sense of continuity with an irretrievably lost psychoanalytic community for its editors, contributors and readers. *The Psychoanalytic Study of the Child* was a "transitional space" (Winnicott, 1953) where the expansion and transformation of the theoretical and clinical legacy of prewar psychoanalysis was undertaken and sustained by its sense of connection with this lost community. In the 1950s, the power of this nostalgic longing was expressed at several meetings where analysts identified with the work of the journal came together. Thus, Ernst Kris opened the Anna Freud Meeting in Stockbridge, Massachusetts, in April of 1950 by expressing the hope that "the spirit of the old can revived here for a few short hours" (Kris, 1951).

The founders of *The Psychoanalytic Study of the Child* declared that "the future of society would depend on the capacity of our children to withstand the ever-mounting tensions in the world of today." They wrote those words against the backdrop of war, exile and loss – experiences that mark the emotional and intellectual lives of so many analysts engaged with the creation of *The Psychoanalytic Study of the Child*. Today, one often hears the question of why émigré analysts so infrequently wrote about their experiences of dislocation and trauma. Perhaps the answer to this question has always been before us and the question is rather why we did not grasp the nature and resiliency of their response.

Bulletin of Information to be Supplied Only to Psychoanalysts Who Desire to Emigrate to the U.S.A.

1. The practice of psychoanalysis in the treatment of adults has been defined legally as the practice of medicine wherever this question has been raised in any law court in this country. Under the Constitution of the United States, however, many legal decisions apply only to the States in which the decision has been given. Although the question has not as yet been subjected to legal testing throughout the country, there can be little doubt that the same decision will ultimately be reached in every State. Therefore, any psychoanalyst who wishes to settle in this country must realize that in practicing psychoanalysis he will be practicing medicine and he will have to subject himself to the conditions under medicine can legally be practiced in the community in which he lives. These conditions are described below.

   The situation with regard to the practice of child-analysis is not yet clear. There is some possibility that the analysis of children will not be looked upon exclusively as the practice of medicine – but that it may be looked upon also as part of the general field of pedagogy. Therefore child analysis may be a field in which properly trained laymen can function without violation of the law. Discreet efforts are being made to clarify this situation at present; but nothing final can be said about it as yet.

   It must be clearly understood, however, that the practice of psychoanalysis on adults without a medical license and a medical degree is a violation of the law for which severe penalties have sometimes been imposed.

2. It is necessary therefore to take legal steps to secure a license for the practice of medicine before practicing psychoanalysis. Licenses to practice medicine are issued by the State of the United States in which one resides. At present, however, there are twenty-one individual States in

the United States in which it is either legally, or for practical reasons, impossible for a foreigner to secure a license to practice medicine. These States are: Arkansas, Delaware, the District of Columbia, Florida, Georgia, Illinois, Kansas, Kentucky, Louisiana, Michigan, Minnesota, Mississippi, Nebraska, Nevada, New Jersey, New Mexico, Pennsylvania, South Dakota, Tennessee, Utah, and Vermont. In some of these States this is because one must become a citizen before one can take the examinations, which would take six years. In others, it is because one must obtain a degree from an American medical school before one can take the examination. In others, it is because one must take one year's internship in an approved hospital before taking the examination. In four States of those listed (namely, Illinois, New Jersey, Pennsylvania and Vermont), the only obstacle to taking the examination is the requirement that the applicant must spend one year in a hospital. Where such a position is obtainable, this of course is not an insurmountable barrier; and although it delays the securing of a license by one year, these four States can be added to the list of available States as possible <u>future</u> homes.

It may also be borne in mind for future use that it is sometimes possible to secure a license in a State where one of those restrictions exist, – and that after practicing in that State for some time (usually a few years are required), it may be possible to have one's license transferred by special arrangement to a nearby State where the original restrictions are more difficult. Obviously, however, this offers no immediate solution to our problem. Therefore, the States in which foreigners may take examinations <u>immediately</u> are: Alaska, Alabama, Arkansas, California, Colorado, Connecticut, Idaho, Indiana, Iowa, Maine, Maryland, Massachusetts, Missouri, Montana, New Hampshire, New York, North Carolina, North Dakota, Ohio, Oklahoma, Oregon, Rhode Island, South Carolina, Texas, Virginia, Washington, West Virginia, Wisconsin, Wyoming.

And in addition, after a one-year internship, Illinois, New Jersey, Pennsylvania and Vermont become available.

3. In every State in which foreigners are permitted at all to take the examinations for a medical license, it is now necessary for the applicant, (no matter how eminent he has been, and no matter how many years he has been practicing in his own country), to pass the written examination which is required of graduates of American medical schools. This examination must be taken in English.

All of these legal facts mean that in order to become established in the practice of psychoanalysis a newcomer may have to be dependent in no small part upon the support which others are able to provide, for some time.

4. Selection of a home in this country, it is important to bear in mind that there are a few large communities in which active centers for the training of psychoanalysts now exist, and in which large bodies of students are already being trained; so that in some of these the field has already become overcrowded. Therefore the newcomers must be prepared to go to other communities where there is a growing demand for well-trained psychoanalysts, but where neither the medical profession nor the lay-public is well informed as yet as to what the practice of psychoanalysis means. Here the newcomer will of necessity have to be prepared to face a certain amount of isolation and loneliness. This is all the more true because psychoanalytic practice, like all other medical practice, is affected seriously at present by the severe economic depression which is felt everywhere.

5. In these difficulties our colleagues from abroad can expect that this Committee will assist them to the best of its ability with advice and with financial support where possible. On the other hand, it is expected that the people to whom help is extended will be ready to pledge themselves to cooperate with us in the following ways:

(a) First that they will be ready to go to communities in which openings are prepared for them, and to look upon their relationship to these communities as real obligations. It is important that they should be prepared to remain there for some years, even though the situation may in some ways be difficulty. (Unless special conditions arise which the Committee agrees would make an immediate change wise and necessary).

This point is stressed because in the past we have had many experiences in which immigrants to this country have made quick and sudden changes in their plans, have sometimes abandoned analyses already begun, and have failed to live up to promises made to physicians and to the community where they have settled. Where this happens, it leaves the community deeply disturbed, and it makes it almost impossible to place any other analyst in that community for a long time to come.

(b) Furthermore, it is expected that all immigrants will present their credentials to some one of the constituent societies of the American Psychoanalytic Association, applying for membership in that Society, and abiding by all of the regulations of that Society.

(c) It is particularly expected that no immigrant, no matter what status he has had in Europe as a training analyst, will undertake to train psychoanalysts independently of one of our established training institutes. In America all training in psychoanalysis is recognized as a function exclusively of those training institutes which are recognized by the American Psychoanalytic Association. We are particularly insistent that this regulation be adhered to by all of our colleagues as they come to settle in this country.

(d) The teaching of psychoanalysis is not the practice of psychoanalysis; and just as laymen may teach in medical schools, so laymen may teach in psychoanalytic institutes provided they are adequately prepared. For those incoming analysts, therefore, who have had sufficient training and experience to be entitled to the rank of Instructor in a recognized training institute, it may be possible to arrange for them to do some preparatory (didactic) analyses even before they have a license to practice. Where this is possible, it will lessen the economic struggle considerably. Even where such analysts are living in a city at some distance from the Institute, it may be possible for them to arrange to function as a part of the teaching staff of that Institute, training carefully chosen students under the auspices and under the regulations of the Institute with which they are affiliated.

6. We hope to be able to grant to well-trained laymen the status of "Honorary Guests" in our Societies. Laymen, however, who expect support from our Committee must agree not to practice psychoanalysis, but to do other work to which we will try to assist them. As explained above, however, it is probable that in the case of child-analysts, work can be done in close contact with and under the supervision of physicians, or under the aegis of some educational institutions. Lay child-analysts must not, however, train laymen for child-analysis without the express permission of the societies of which they are guests.

7. The securing of visas and affidavits: In order to secure permission to come to this country to live permanently, it is necessary for a foreigner to secure a visa at the nearest consular office. Under the existing law, the

Consul is not permitted to give this visa unless the prospective immigrant can give evidence that he has money enough to live for a sufficient length of time to get established independently in this country. If he has not money, or if the country which he is leaving will not permit him to bring money with him, he must have an affidavit issued by someone in this country.

This affidavit is a promise to support the incoming individual, and not allow him to every become a public charge. Naturally such affidavits can be given only by people of means. The government requires that evidence be given of the income of the guarantors, and in certain cases requires that money or securities be placed on deposit. The specific requirements vary with the number of dependents in the family of the foreigner who is coming over, with the likelihood of his getting work in his particular profession, etc. Naturally friends and relatives of incoming foreigners are more ready to give such affidavits than are strangers. Nevertheless, it is sometimes possible to secure such affidavits from generous-minded strangers. In order to do so, however, we need the fullest possible information on the individual who wants to come to this country. For this reason, in additional to its usefulness in helping to secure positions for our colleagues from abroad, we are enclosing a questionnaire which we would like to have filled out in full by every individual who wants to come to America.

Curriculum Vitae

1. Name, address, age.
2. Place of birth – citizenship – how and when acquired.
3. If married, Name, address, age, place of birth and citizenship of husband or wife.
4. If married, the occupation of the wife or husband.
5. Number of dependents – names, ages, married or single.
6. Degree of command of English and other languages.
7. General education: (Complete record of school, university, and scientific training – where studies were carried out, dates, under what particular outstanding teachers any special training was received, all degrees received – where and when).
8. Medical training: Medical school record, record of all types of hospital experience both general and psychiatric, out-patient clinic experience, etc. with dates and places.

9. Academic ranks held – teaching positions, lectureships, etc.
10. Psychoanalytic training: Preparatory analysis, where and when and by whom, duration; in what Psychoanalytic Institute studies were pursued (with details); under whom supervised work was conducted, etc.
11. If applicant has been a teacher in any psychoanalytic institute, – what teaching has been conducted, what courses given, what supervisory work has been carried on, etc.
12. List of most important scientific publications or publications in any academic or intellectual field.
13. Full data on all types of special experience or training in non-analytic fields, which might lead to opportunities for teaching or other work. With regard to this, it is important to give as full details as possible.
14. Send this information to:

Lawrence S. Kubie, Chairman
Emergency Committee on Relief and Immigration
34 East 75th Street
New York

Notes

1 This paper draws on two earlier publications (Thompson, 2012; Thompson and Keable, 2016).
2 The paper Deutsch refers to in her letter was published later that year with the title, "Some forms of emotional disturbance and their relationship to schizophrenia." It remains a major clinical contribution to the understanding of the "as if" personality (Thompson, 1987).

References

Deutsch, H. (1942). Unpublished Letter to Raymond Gosselin, June 12. Papers of The Psychoanalytic Quarterly, A.A. Brill Library, Archives and Special Collections, New York Psychoanalytic Society and Institute.

Kris, E. (1951). Opening Remarks on Psychoanalytic Child Psychology. *Psychoanalytic Study of the Child* 6:9–17.

Kubie, L. (1938a). The Emergency Committee on Relief and Immigration of the American Psychoanalytic Association, March 19, 1938. Archives, A.A. Brill Library, New York Psychoanalytic Society and Institute.

Kubie, L. (1938b). Report of the Emergency Committee on Relief and Immigration. March 31, 1938, Archives, A.A. Brill Library, New York Psychoanalytic Society and Institute.

Kubie, L. (1938c). Unpublished Letter to Ernest Jones, April 26, 1938. Archives, A.A. Brill Library, New York Psychoanalytic Society and Institute.

Neubauer, P. (1986). Panelist, "The Experience of Migration," Oral History Workshop #25, December 18, 1986, American Psychoanalytic Association, New York, NY.

Thompson, N.L. (1987). Helene Deutsch: A Life in Theory. *The Psychoanalytic Quarterly* LVI:317–353.

Thompson, N.L. (2012). The Transformation of Psychoanalysis in America: Émigré Analysts and the New York Psychoanalytic Society and Institute, 1935–1961. *Journal of the American Psychoanalytic Association* 60:9–44.

Thompson, N.L. (2014). Ernst Kris in America. *American Imago* 71:353–374.

Thompson, N.L. and Keable, H. (2016). The Psychoanalytic Study of the Child: A Narrative of Postwar Psychoanalysis. *American Imago* 73:343–365.

Warburg, B. (1948). Summary of the Work of the Emergency Committee on Relief and Immigration of the American Psychoanalytic Association, 1938–1948. Unpublished. Archives, American Psychoanalytic Association. Oskar Diethelm Library, Weill Cornell Medical College.

Warburg, B. (1976). Summary of the Work of the Emergency Committee on Relief and Immigration of the American Psychoanalytic Association. Unpublished. Prepared for the Research Foundation for Jewish Immigration, Inc. Archives, American Psychoanalytic Association. Oskar Diethelm Library, Weill Cornell Medical College.

Winnicott, D.W. (1953). Transitional Objects and Transitional Phenomena: A Study of the First Not-Me Possession. *International Journal of Psychoanalysis* 34:89–97.

Chapter 2

Émigré Psychoanalysis in the Age of McCarthyism

Ellen Schrecker

During the 1940s and 1950s, just as the émigré psychoanalysts were coming to terms with the losses incurred by their forced departure from Europe and the need to reestablish their lives and livelihoods in a new country, the nation that so ambivalently welcomed them was about to undergo what came to be known as McCarthyism – the most widespread and longest lasting episode of political repression in its history.

Before we try to assess how that wave of political repression may (or may not) have affected the European psychoanalysts, it would help to clear up some of the main myths that still cloud our understanding of that repression.[1] It is unfortunate that it was named for an individual who came late to the party, for Joseph McCarthy did not appear on the scene until early in 1950, a few years after the movement to which he gave his name had gotten under way. In fact, if we knew then what we know now, we might have called that movement Hooverism, after FBI Director J. Edgar Hoover, who more than any other single individual created the ideology and infrastructure of the anti-Communist crusade of the early Cold War.

Whatever name we want to give it, McCarthyism became the key component of the home front of the early Cold War. It was not a random wave of repression, it was very specifically directed against Communism. And it was designed to eliminate the American Communist party (CP) and all the individuals, organizations, and ideas associated with it from any position of influence within American life. With only a few exceptions, its victims were not "innocent liberals," but members and former members of the Communist party, as well as those individuals who did not join the CP but were nonetheless active within its penumbra, the so-called "fellow travelers." Significantly, although McCarthyism was not specifically designed to repress political dissent, because of the way in which the Communist "enemy" was defined, that was, in fact, what happened.

DOI: 10.4324/9781003266228-4

American Communism in Context

It is important to realize that, to a certain extent, American Communism shaped the measures used against it. As a result, to understand how the political repression of the McCarthy era operated, we need to look beyond the demonized stereotypes of American Communists prevalent during the early years of the Cold War. Once we do that, we will encounter a deeply flawed movement that, for a few years during the 1930s and 1940s, was the most dynamic force for social change within the American Left. Its strengths and its defects influenced the campaign against it, thus determining at least in part that campaign's impact on the rest of American society.

Unpopular from the start, the American Communist party faced repression throughout its history. Organized at the end of World War I, it spent much of the 1920s as an illegal, underground organization. Comprised mainly of immigrants, it held the Soviet franchise as the official American representative of the Bolshevik Revolution. That connection was both detrimental and beneficial for the CP. It did get some financial support from Moscow that probably allowed the tiny and beleaguered group to survive in an inhospitable environment. But at the same time, its dependence on and allegiance to the Soviet Union forced the party's leaders to defer to the Kremlin's interests, a practice that not only promoted an unrealistic view of American politics but also destroyed any hope of internal democracy. And, when the Cold War broke out in the late 1940s, the party's ties to the Soviet Union rendered it vulnerable to the all-too-plausible charge that it was undermining U.S. national security.

An equally deleterious problem was that because of the repression directed against it, the CP expected its members to keep their affiliation a secret. That was a serious mistake. It created an aura of conspiracy around the group that made its members seem as if they were involved with some clandestine revolutionary plot. That secrecy became particularly counterproductive during the McCarthy era because it enabled anti-Communists to rely on the tactic of exposure as a mechanism of repression.

For most of the 1920s, the small, clandestine party was torn by infighting. During the 1930s, however, spurred by the Great Depression and the rise of fascism, it grew into what became the most dynamic group on the Left. Although it was never to have more than about 100,000 members, it attracted a unique generation of idealists and activists who threw themselves into the many causes that the Communist party was backing. They

organized labor unions, resisted fascism, fought for racial equality, and supported most of the New Deal's social and economic reforms. It owed its
effectiveness to its members' energetic participation in the broader political
movement of the 1930s and 1940s known as the Popular Front. Unions
were the most important elements of the Popular Front that the Communists worked with, but there were also cultural and professional groups,
anti-fascist organizations concerned about the Spanish Civil War, summer
camps, literary magazines, and literally dozens of other groups that, for a
few years, allowed the CP to create an entire left-wing world for its members and sympathizers. One man I wrote about recalled that he once went
to 34 meetings in one week. Unfortunately, when McCarthyism emerged,
involvement with those groups could prove disastrous.

The Communist party had a lot of enemies. Not just conservatives,
though they were certainly crucial to the Cold War Red Scare, but also the
Catholic church, Trotskyists, and other groups of ex-Communists as well
as other rivals on the Left and even liberals who found party members rigid
and hard to collaborate with in the organizations they both supported. The
CP's most important – certainly its most powerful – antagonists were those
right-wing business leaders, bureaucrats, and politicians who opposed the
New Deal reforms and who fought them by charging that the Roosevelt and
Truman administrations were under Communist influence.

The McCarthy era scenario of Communists in the government was
already gaining currency by the end of the 1930s. It lost momentum during World War II when the United States and the Soviet Union were allied
against Hitler. Although still unpopular, the Communist party was tolerated
during the war and many of its members even worked for the government.
A few, as we now know, also engaged in espionage for the Russians that
included supplying information about the atomic bomb.

Once the war ended, the Red Scare resumed. Only this time, the advent
of the Cold War between the United States and the Soviet Union transformed Communism from an unpopular political movement into a threat to
national security. That transformation thrust the anti-Communist crusade
into the mainstream of American domestic politics where it was embraced
by conservative politicians eager to roll back the New Deal. Such was
especially the case after the 1948 presidential election when Truman's surprise victory made the Republican party desperate to find a new issue since
its opposition to the New Deal's domestic reforms had not found favor with
the voters.

Enter McCarthyism. It enabled the Republicans to attack the Democratic administration by charging that the Roosevelt and Truman administrations had been riddled with Communists who were undermining America's position in the world. There was some plausibility – albeit enormously exaggerated – to those charges, but whatever influence party members may have had during World War II had disappeared within a year or two after it ended. Even so, the plausibility of the partisan charge that the Democrats were "soft on Communism" threw the Truman administration and its liberal supporters onto the defensive. Because they never publicly questioned the exaggerated scenario of the Communist danger that was being purveyed by right-wing ideologues like the FBI's J. Edgar Hoover and the members of the House Un-American Activities Committee (HUAC), they were unable to keep the witch hunt within bounds as they struggled to prove they were at least as devoted to purging Reds as their critics. All too often, these mainstream liberals not only did not oppose repressive measures against supposed subversives, but even collaborated with them, imposing their own anti-Communist investigations and blacklists.

Accordingly, when the Cold War escalated in the late 1940s and early 1950s at a moment when the Communist revolution triumphed in China, the Soviet Union detonated a nuclear weapon, and the Korean War broke out, the notion that American Communists in the government and elsewhere had betrayed their county to Moscow and might do so again gained enormous political traction. It undergirded the political repression that was to dominate U.S. domestic politics for nearly a decade.

The Cold War Red Scare and the Émigré Psychoanalysts

As the McCarthy era red scare swept through American society, the émigré psychoanalysts were just finding their personal and professional footing in their new country. As far as I can tell, however, they seem to have not been affected much, if at all, by the anti-Communist purges. Since it is hard for historians to write about things that did not happen, I can only speculate about the reasons why the psychoanalytic community may have been spared the ravages of the Cold War Red Scare.

Probably the most important reason is that they were not involved with the Communist party or with the kinds of left-wing political activities that would have attracted the attention of the anti-Communist witch hunters. Whether or not that was because the psychoanalytical movement itself was inherently depoliticizing is a subject I am unequipped to deal with. However, what seems to have been the case was that the émigrés had at least already eschewed left-wing political activity before McCarthyism emerged. Hitler had been a much greater threat to them than the House Un-American Activities Committee or J. Edgar Hoover would ever be. As Russell Jacoby describes the situation, the political Freudians within the group of émigré psychoanalysts around Otto Fenichel had largely abandoned their earlier political radicalism as they struggled for survival and fled from Europe to the United States.[2] After their arrival, many seemed to have felt enormous gratitude to their new country. Erik Erikson was probably typical in that regard, calling the United States "a loving stepfather in an adopted country."[3]

The second reason why the émigré psychoanalysts escaped the direct impact of McCarthyism has to do with the nature of psychoanalysis as a profession. Its practitioners were what we would call today "independent contractors," and thus immune to the economic sanctions that made McCarthyism so successful. We can safely assume that their patients were not sympathetic to the Red Scare and would not have participated in blacklisting its victims.

Although McCarthyism was remarkably effective in eliminating left-wing dissent in the United States, unlike political repression in other societies, it did not rely upon the use of violence or coercion by the state. Only two people were killed (Julius and Ethel Rosenberg), several hundred were sent to prison, and several thousand lost their jobs. The Cold War Red Scare's main sanctions were economic. The supposed Communists, who were its main victims, lost their jobs and were blacklisted – the threat of unemployment proving every bit as effective in crushing political dissent as imprisoning people or assassinating them.

The economic sanctions that made McCarthyism so powerful operated in accordance with a two-stage procedure. First, the targeted individuals were identified as Communists, usually by an official body like a congressional investigating committee or the FBI. Then, they were fired. It was common at the time to view McCarthyism primarily as its first stage of exposing supposed Communists. As a result, many of the liberals and moderates who ran the movie studios, universities, industrial corporations, and government bureaucracies that operated the second stage by firing and refusing to hire the men and women identified during the first stage of the Red Scare were able to distance themselves from the political implications of their actions.

In fact, because they often deplored the bizarre behavior of Senator McCarthy and some of his allies, it was easier for the managers of the public or private institutions or corporations to justify applying the economic sanctions that made McCarthyism so effective. They did so, either because they bought into the prevalent demonization of supposed Communists as political robots under Stalin's control and, thus, genuinely believed that the men and women identified by the FBI or the House Un-American Activities Committee deserved to be fired or else, as was common among moderates and liberals, because they feared that their companies and institutions, not to mention their own careers, could be damaged if they kept the tainted individuals on their payrolls.

But most psychoanalysts were not employees. Because their economic livelihood depended on individual arrangements with their patients, they were not as susceptible to blacklisting as people in other fields. The only major institutions that they would have had contact with were hospitals and universities. And, although I know of a few physicians who were called before congressional committees and then fired and blacklisted, I don't know if any were psychoanalysts, let alone European émigrés. Nor, except for the people I will mention in the following, do I know of any academic psychoanalysts who were affected. Were there blacklists within the field? I simply don't know, nor do I know to what extent McCarthyism had an impact on the medical, let alone the psychiatric, profession.

If there has been any systematic research on that subject, I am unaware of it. It could be a challenging project. People involved with the anti-Communist purges, whether the victims or the perpetrators, tended to keep that involvement secret if they could. Accordingly, even though I have found a few instances where members of the émigré psychoanalytical community did have brushes with McCarthyism, I have no idea if there were any others.

What seems to have been the case, however, is that the profession of psychoanalysis withstood the witch hunt rather well. It actually enabled a few individuals barred from other professions to avoid the blacklist and reestablish themselves in a new career. But, again, there is research to be done. The most we can say is that McCarthyism wasn't completely absent from the lives of the émigré psychoanalysts, even if indirectly.

Wilhelm Reich was by far the most persecuted of the émigrés during the McCarthy years. But his troubles, though devastating, had little direct relationship to the anti-Communist purges. As his mental health deteriorated during the 1950s and he became increasingly paranoid in defense of his so-called orgone boxes, the Food and Drug Administration cracked down on him for fraud. Convicted and sentenced to a two-year prison term, he died of a heart attack in the Lewisburg Federal Penitentiary in 1956. But, despite his earlier involvement with Communism, the punitive treatment that he received at the hands of the United States government was not explicitly political in a way that could be characterized as McCarthyist. Still, the constricted political-cum-cultural atmosphere of the 1950s that allowed Reich's admittedly aberrant behavior to be criminalized certainly owes something to the "black silence of fear" that Supreme Court Justice William O. Douglas observed casting its pall over American society at the time.[4]

A more direct connection can be made, however, to one of the most well-known episodes of McCarthyism: the University of California loyalty oath crisis of 1949–50. One of the earliest manifestations of the anti-Communist political tests for employment that characterized the Cold War Red Scare, the 1949 oath required all University of California faculty members to sign a disclaimer that they did not belong to the Communist party or any other organization that sought to overthrow the government by force or violence. Its repressive function was obvious, especially since no other state employees had to subscribe to such a measure. Understandably, it threw the University of California's professors into turmoil for more than a year as they agonized over whether to sign.[5]

Two émigré analysts were caught up in it: Else Frenkel-Brunswick and Erik Erikson. Neither wanted to sign. But, like all but about 30 faculty holdouts, they both ultimately gave in. Frenkel-Brunswick did so because she wanted to continue her work with Theodor Adorno on the project that led to *The Authoritarian Personality*.[6] Erikson was seriously conflicted. He decided to resign from his teaching position on the faculty because he felt that he would be betraying his students if he were to "participate without protest in a vague, fearful, and vindictive gesture devised to ban an evil in some magical way." However, he later quietly sent a non-Communist disclaimer in a letter to the regents because he, too, wanted to keep his research position at Berkeley.[7]

Epilogue: Psychoanalysis and the Academic Blacklist

Significantly, however – and I'm not sure whether this is known within the psychoanalytic community – just as most of the European émigrés were eventually able to integrate themselves into the American profession, so, too, was it possible for a handful of academic victims of McCarthyism to carve out a living beyond the blacklist by becoming lay analysts. I know of at least five such individuals, most, but not all, of them psychologists – two of whom actually ended up teaching at the New School.

The Communist party did not officially allow its members to seek psychotherapy. Freudianism's emphasis on the individual psyche was seen as an unwelcome challenge to the party's collectivist mindset, while psychoanalysis' requirement of complete honesty threatened the secrecy that the party demanded of its members. Still, people on the Left were not immune to the need for psychotherapy, especially at a time when their past and present politics made them vulnerable to political repression and its economic consequences. Accordingly, they sought out sympathetic therapists who could be trusted, the defrocked professors among them. After all, as victims of the witch hunt who had destroyed their academic careers by standing up to the Cold War inquisition, the blacklisted professors had clearly passed a left-wing version of a political test for employment. And, in fact, they seem to have had few problems attracting patients and supporting themselves as lay analysts.[8]

Ralph Gundlach was one of the earliest and most eminent of these blacklisted academics. Although he may well have been too ornery to have joined the CP, he was a key activist in Seattle's vibrant Popular Front community until McCarthyism hit. An associate professor of psychology at the University of Washington, he was also a prolific scholar, recognized as such within his field where he served as president of the Western Psychological Society. Along with half a dozen other Washington faculty members, he had refused to cooperate with the state's anti-Communist Canwell Committee in 1948 and was to serve a short prison sentence for contempt. He was equally unwilling to cooperate with the University of Washington's internal investigation of his political activities. As a result, Gundlach was fired in the beginning of 1949 along with two other professors who had admitted to party membership in what became the first important academic freedom case of the early Cold War. Blacklisted, he moved to New York City, where he continued to do research and publish while establishing himself as a lay analyst.[9]

Harry Slochower was another professor who continued his scholarly career after he lost his job teaching German and comparative literature at Brooklyn College. In an appearance before Nevada senator Pat McCarran's Senate Internal Security Subcommittee (SISS) in November of 1952,

Slochower took the Fifth Amendment about his political past. Because he had been identified as a party member during an anti-Communist investigation by New York State's so-called Rapp-Coudert Committee ten years before, Slochower had long expected he might be fired. As a result, he had been retraining himself as a lay analyst and was even seeing patients before his bout with McCarran ended his career at Brooklyn College. He did not abandon scholarship, however, and remained immersed in examining the cultural and artistic ramifications of psychoanalysis while also serving as editor of *American Imago*, the main journal in that field, as well as teaching at the New School for Social Research.[10]

Several other New York City academics who refused to cooperate with the same set of SISS investigations as Slochower had followed the same trajectory. Bernard Reiss, an associate professor of psychology at Hunter College, had also appeared before the Rapp-Coudert Committee and, expecting a replay after World War II, had begun training at the Postgraduate Center for Mental Health. Within a few months after he, too, was fired for taking the Fifth, he was able to support himself as a lay analyst and the research director of a large mental health clinic. He also ended up teaching at the New School.[11]

Another academic victim of the McCarran committee's 1952 hearings was Edwin Berry Burgum, who taught English at New York University. Fired the following year, Burgum also retrained himself as a lay analyst. Although he admitted that he made two times as much money as a psychotherapist as he had as a college teacher, Burgum found that it was hard to adjust to the instability of his income within his new profession.[12]

On the West Coast, there was Harry Steinmetz, a psychology professor at San Diego State College, who was fired in 1954 after having taken the Fifth Amendment before the HUAC the previous year. After attempting to evade the blacklist by taking on a few temporary teaching positions, Steinmetz switched careers and became a lay analyst, practicing in San Diego and Los Angeles.[13]

In an ironic twist, a Hollywood psychotherapist was forced out of the profession because he had collaborated with McCarthyism. Philip Cohen had once been in the Communist party; and, as a result, he was sought out by many of the Communists and former Communists in the film industry who were being hauled before the inquisition. In the guise of therapy, he convinced some of them to cooperate with the committees and the FBI. Naming names would, he supposedly claimed, make their own lives better.

Nevertheless, once his behavior became known within the Los Angeles Left, his practice was ruined and he left the field.[14]

* * * *

Ultimately, if we are to assess the impact of McCarthyism on the émigré psychoanalysts, we must look more at what did *not* happen than at what did. Self-censorship is a large part of the story. It was certainly common among the academics I studied. One outstanding scholar of American culture told me, for example, that during the McCarthy era, he never used the word "capitalism" in his work. "Industrialism" was the term of choice. Similarly, the psychologist Leon Kamin, who had taken the Fifth in front of McCarthy, studied rats for years until he felt safe enough to embark on debunking the supposed genetic basis of human intelligence.

Did that kind of self-censorship occur within the field of psychoanalysis? Did the field impose political tests for employment upon its practitioners? And were the émigré analysts involved? Perhaps some future scholar can find the answers, or at least open up the discussion.

Notes

1 For the fuller discussion of McCarthyism from which I have drawn for this article, see Ellen Schrecker, *Many Are the Crimes: McCarthyism in America* (New York and Boston: Little, Brown and Company, 1998) and ibid., *No Ivory Tower: McCarthyism and the Universities* (New York: Oxford University Press, 1986).

2 Russell Jacoby, *The Repression of Pscyhoanalysis: Otto Fenichel and the Political Freudians* (New York: Basic Books, 1983).

3 Paul Roazen, *Erik H. Erikson: The Power and Limits of a Vision* (New York: The Free Press, 1976), 93.

4 William O. Douglas, The Black Silence of Fear. *New York Times Magazine*, January 13, 1952, in Ellen Schrecker, *The Age of McCarthyism: A Brief History with Documents* (New York: Bedford Books of St. Martin's Press, 1994), 243–246.

5 The best recent study of the California Loyalty oath is Bob Blauner, *Resisting McCarthyism: To Sign or Not to Sign California's Loyalty Oath* (Stanford: Stanford University Press, 2009). See also David P. Gardner, *The California Oath Crisis* (Berkeley: University of California Press, 1967).

6 Blauner, *Resisting McCarthyism*, 280.

7 Blauner, Ibid., 140, 171; Paul Roazen, *Erik H. Erikson: The Power and Limits of a Vision* (New York: Free Press, 1976).

8 On Communism and psychoanalysis, see Victor S. Navasky, *Naming Names* (New York: Viking, 1980), 131–143; Schrecker, *No Ivory Tower*, 284.

 9 For the University of Washington case, see Vern Countryman, *Un-American Activities in the State of Washington* (Ithaca: Cornell University Press, 1951).
10 Schrecker, *No Ivory Tower*, 170–171, 284–285.
11 David Caute, *The Great Fear: The Anti-Communist Purge under Truman and Eisenhower* (New York: Simon and Schuster, 1978), 552–553.
12 Ibid.
13 Ibid., 553; Home >> Special Collections & University Archives >> Raising Our Voices: The History of San Diego State and San Diego in Sound >> San Diego State University History >> Faculty Oral Histories & Recordings >> Harry Steinmetz <https://library.sdsu.edu/scua/raising-our-voices/sdsu-history/faculty/harry-steinmetz>
14 Navasky, *Naming Names*, 131–143.

Chapter 3

The Saga of the Budapest School of Psychoanalysis

Double Exile[1]

Judit Mészáros

The Budapest School of psychoanalysis faced *two forced exiles within 20 years* between the 1920s and the early 1940s. The first exile happened soon after the First World War, when a Bolshevik-type of revolution and counterrevolution, political retribution, and surge of anti-Semitism pushed Hungary's outstanding intellectuals and promising future professionals to leave the country (Frank, 2009). A significant part of the small Hungarian Psychoanalytical Society and many from the next psychoanalytic generation emigrated mainly to Vienna and Berlin (Mészáros, 2014).

Among them were Sandor Rado, Sandor Lorand, Melanie Klein, Margaret Mahler, Michael and Alice Balint, Franz Alexander, Therese Benedek, and René Spitz. Most of them joined the Berlin Society. The first psychoanalyst from Hungary to go to New York, Sandor Lorand, had asked for Ferenczi's help with contacts there. He arrived at the New York Psychoanalytic Society in the mid-1920s. His prophecy, "I don't see the possibility of a peaceful life here in the future"[2] had unfortunately come true.

Exile from Europe

The second exile of the Hungarian psychoanalysts began soon after the *Anschluss* – annexation of Austria. Soon after, the Hungarian Parliament passed the first anti-Jewish law in the spring of 1938. I would just like to emphasize that Hungary was not occupied by the Third Reich at that time and was not occupied for many years, until March 1944. The first anti-Jewish law restricted options for Jews in liberal professions by cutting to 20 percent the number of Jewish members tied to the press, theatre, law, medicine, and business. The "second Jewish law" a year later, which further

DOI: 10.4324/9781003266228-5

restricted the Jews in public life and business, determined Jewish identity based on *race* in the spirit of Germany's Nuremberg Laws.

During the second exile, some who had returned after a previous emigration left the country once again, including Alice and Michael Balint, Edith Gyömrői, and, soon afterward, Robert Bak, Sandor Feldmann, and David Rapaport.

Among the Budapest psychoanalysts, the Balints and Geza Roheim wanted to resettle in London. For Roheim, who was an ethnographer and the founder of psychoanalytic anthropology, it was essential to remain a part of European culture. Two weeks after the Anschluss, Roheim sent a request to John Rickman.

My dear John!   28. III. [March] 1938

Of course Vienna comes first, I knew that, it is quite obvious. The point is that everybody is trying to get away from here before something happens, and it may be too late. . . . Maybe this is only a group psychosis but one never knows. Now there is just one thing you can do for me. Please let me have a fictive invitation to give lectures at the Institute of Psychoanalysis say for a year, so that I can use this if I want an English [visa] suddenly. . . . Thanks at any rate and I quite understand about the Vienna people.

With kindest regards to you both,
Yours ever,
Géza

Why Was Roheim's Request Refused?
Why Not London – Ernest Jones

Jones, who had always maintained a rivalry with Ferenczi, sent him red rose bushes for the garden of his new villa in Budapest. At the same time, Jones's "poisoned thorns" had a crippling effect on the spread of Ferenczi's ideas for decades after his death. Indeed, Jones spread the rumor that Ferenczi had been suffering from paranoia, so, despite denials by contemporaries who knew Ferenczi well, including Roheim and Michael Balint, Jones wished to keep analysts who were close to Ferenczi far away from London. That is precisely why the Balints could resettle in Manchester with John

Rickman's help in early 1939, but Roheim was forced to switch continents to find a new home due to Jones's persistent refusals.

At the same time, Jones was instrumental in helping the Hungarian analysts find their way to other continents. For example, it was through Jones that Edith Gyömrői resettled in Ceylon (now Sri Lanka) and Clara Lazar Gero found a home in Melbourne, where she established the Melbourne Psychoanalytic Group in 1941.

István Hollós, the president of the Hungarian Psychoanalytic Society, turned to Lawrence S. Kubie, the chair of the *Emergency Committee on Relief and Immigration* (ECRI), in early 1939.

Dear Kubie,

During the Paris meeting in August, 1939, I communicated to our colleagues that our Hungarian members had decided to stay under every possible circumstances in their country, and so continue their work here, as far as that is possible. . . .

Though our recent situation is not yet so difficult, but its turn to the worst can be expected in a very short time [emphasis added]. I made the same statement to Dr. Jones as well and he gave me the advice in his very encouraging and detailed letter, to let also you know the present condition . . . to consider our difficult situation . . . and ask you to inform us about the possibilities, difficulties and the means ways we should try. A list of about 15 persons will be too sent to you for your disposition.

Believe me sincerely
Yours
Dr. Hollós[3]

I would like to highlight some aspects of the operation of the ECRI and about the political and professional difficulties it faced.

The ECRI of the American Psychoanalytic Association: 1938–1948 – Ten Years that Changed the History of Psychoanalysis

On March 13, 1938, one day after the Anschluss, the American Psychoanalytic Association (APsaA) set up the ECRI.[4] We all know that the

psychoanalytic movement has been influenced by personal and professional antagonisms, envy, and rivalries, from the outset. However, when
the Americans established the ECRI in New York during a historical period,
we saw something else: a complete change and shift in priorities. They
pushed the antagonism into the background and placed the saving of lives
in the foreground.

The ECRI was a small committee with huge influence in the history of
psychoanalysis. The 14 members represented the four component societies of the APsaA (Jeffrey, 1989; Mészáros, 1998, 2012; Thompson, 2012),
and most of them were credible representatives of the European analysts,
since they had considerable experience with and personal ties to their European colleagues. They had a good understanding of what was going on in
Europe, and many of them had had training analysis in Berlin. There were
the two who were originally from Hungary, Rado and Alexander, who were
invited to the US at the beginning of the 1930s, and also Thomas French
and Bertram D. Lewin, both of whom had been trained by Alexander at the
Berlin Institute.

The committee chair, Lawrence S. Kubie, had spent several years in London, while Helene Deutsch's own life history made her very much at home
in Central Eastern Europe. She knew the members of both the Vienna and
Berlin societies very well and was familiar with conditions in the region.
She had settled in Boston in 1935. Bettina Warburg was the committee
co-chair, secretary, and much more. She was an extraordinary person and
a motherly figure far beyond her difficult duties. She was the one who
dealt with everything from finding jobs to addressing the émigrés' personal
problems.

**The Emergency Committee on Relief and Immigration of the APsaA
1938–1948**

Chairman: Dr. Lawrence S. Kubie
Co-Chair: Dr. Bettina Warburg
Committee Members
Boston: Dr. Helene Deutsch, Dr. Ralph Kaufman, Dr. Henry Murray
Chicago: Dr. Franz Alexander, Dr. Thomas French
New York: Dr. George Daniels, Dr. Adolf Meyer, Dr. Lawrence Kubie,
   Dr. Bertram Lewin, Dr. Sandor Rado, Dr. Bettina Warburg
Washington-Baltimore: Dr. Lewis Hill

The ECRI Expressed Solidarity, Created Opportunities, and Asked for Cooperation and Personal Responsibility from the Émigrés

The Committee had a "*domestic policy*," a "*foreign policy*," and, to realize both, a "*financial policy*" aimed at organizing fundraising to obtain the financial resources necessary to assist European peers in escaping and resettling.

Kubie was the liaison between the Committee and the State Department. He was in direct contact with the IPA, both through Edward Glover, a leading figure in the IPA from London, and Ernest Jones, who at that time was the president of both the IPA and the British Psychoanalytical Society. It was through the cooperation of these three men that the main emigration strategy was formed for the European psychoanalysts.

It was crucial for financial resources to be made available to the committee, which is why they began fundraising, with financial matters in the capable hands of Lewin.

One of the main duties of the Committee was to generate *affidavits* and find *jobs* to obtain visas. The word *affidavit* took on a magical power. Having it meant yes, a green light to a visa. It had to be proved that an immigrant would not represent a burden on the state, and thus someone had to provide a guarantee and place money on deposit for a year: "for a family of three or four, who could not be expected to earn any material sum of money within a year, they would want a guarantee of about $5,000" (cited in Kurzweil, 1992, p. 344).

That amount was equal to the annual salary of a junior physician or that of the chief administrator at the Chicago Psychoanalytic Institute.

Kubie wrote the following to Hollós about the Hungarians in 1939: "I can assure you that we will do all we can to secure affidavits . . . for all of our colleagues who want ultimately to come here" (Kubie, 1939).

The aims of the ECRI were to provide aid to European psychoanalyst peers and their families in resettling in the US and in rapidly integrating into American society. Unlike most foundations, the aim was not to promote a brain drain, in the sense that the Committee did not provide assistance to only the very best. At the same time, ECRI requested two-way cooperation and efforts. The Committee put together a *Bulletin of Information* about the possibilities – and obligations – involved. For example, the émigrés had to accept, in principle, that they would be resettled in "less developed" areas if they accepted the help of the ECRI. In a letter from Lawrence S. Kubie to Ernest Jones on April 26, 1938, he said:

> Our larger centers, where well organized societies and institutes already exist, are well supplied with trained analysts and students in training; and this number has already been increased by immigrants from Germany. On the other hand, there are many large cities where there is a need for psychoanalysis and where there are literally no psychoanalysts, so those who accept our assistance will cooperate with us and follow our recommendations.

> (*ibid.*)

The principles were clear. At the same time, after a while, these were over-ridden by humanitarian considerations.

The ECRI and the Political Climate Surrounding it – US Immigration Policy

The significance of the ECRI can only be fully appreciated in the context of the US government's refugee and immigration policy, which was characterized by:

1) Restrictive immigration laws and regulations.
2) The rigid attitude of US State Department officials and their overemphasis on protecting American interests.

These two factors clearly reflected the anti-immigration sentiment among the American public. In January of 1939, nine months after the Anschluss, 82% of the population opposed immigration. By the end of March in 1940, over 100 xenophobic proposals and bills had been put before the US Congress (Breitman and Kraut, 1987).

The whole society was infiltrated by *fear, hate*, and *prejudice*. Historically, the White Anglo-Saxon Protestant (WASP) American mainstream lived in fear of ethnic and religious minorities such as "blacks, Orientals, Roman Catholics, as well as Jews" (Breitman and Kraut, 1987, p. 7). The fear of each group was expressed through a different prejudice for the Slavs ("Every Slav is a Bolshevik agitator"), Italians ("Every Italian is an anarchist"), and Jews ("who have too much power in the US"). Antisemitism was also harsh. Of the 48 US states then, *only seven permitted* the settlement of Jewish émigrés.

A quota system was developed in 1921. The system set an annual number for each country in permitting immigrants to settle in the US. For Austria, as an example, the quota was 1,413, even as hundreds of thousands of people faced imminent danger after the Anschluss. The quota system was rigid, and there was no wish to change it. "Vice President John Nance Garner said that, if it were left to a secret vote of Congress, *all* immigration would be stopped. The idea of raising the quota was dropped" (ibid, p. 58). President Roosevelt created a clever compromise for Austrian citizens: the Austrian quota should be added to the German quota, since the country was annexed by Germany, so the potential number of German and Austrian immigrants would be 25,957. For Hungary, the annual quota was around 400. The quota system did not change between 1933 and 1944, and the total number of émigrés did not surpass 54% of the quota.

In the US, there was also a strong fear of the left-wing intelligentsia. George S. Messersmith – the consul general in Berlin – argued as follows in 1933:

> We cannot fill our own universities with foreign professors who are alien to our thought and will influence our youth in a direction not in line with our national policy and our cultural life.
>
> The average Jew, for example, who desires to emigrate to the United States, will be very glad to be able to make a home for himself in our country and to fit himself into our picture; but these professors who feel that they have a mission in life may potentially be a danger to us.
>
> (Letter from Messersmith to Carr, 5 July 1933, cited in Breitman and Kraut, 1987, pp. 44–45)

The University in Exile was proposed by Alvin S. Johnson (1874–1971); it later became part of The New School for Social Research and employed numerous left-wing and Jewish staff who had had to flee Germany immediately after Hitler came to the power.

Soon after, many analysts tried to find a country within Europe to be able to continue their life. A considerable number of the analysts at the Berlin Psychoanalytic Society and Institute escaped to Prague, including, among others, the Freudian leftist/Marxist analysts Frances Deri and Annie Reich; the Viennese Otto Fenichel, who was the charismatic leader of the so-called

"Kinderseminar" (Children's Seminar); and its members, were all obliged to leave Berlin immediately, both because of their Jewish origin and their political inclination. Together with Emanuel Windholz, who was of Slovak descent and had previously been to Prague, they established the Czecho-Slovakian Study Group, which was affiliated with the Vienna Society and was approved by the IPA at the Lucerne congress in 1934. But all of them had been forced to leave Prague within a few years after their emigration from Berlin, just as many analysts had to leave Budapest when anti-Jewish laws came out in Hungary beginning in 1938. Finally, there was no safe place in Europe.

The ECRI did everything to facilitate resettlement, independent of whether the applicant was a lay analyst or not. It was saving members of the psychoanalytic community merely as members of that community. For example, among them was Valerie Reich from Vienna, secretary to a number of psychoanalysts and a typist and translator of scientific works.

Internal Tensions between the IPA and the APsaA

Tensions could be traced back to two earlier factors. One was the effort within American psychoanalysis to become independent and separate itself from European traditions and development, the other was the matter of lay analysis.

In terms of lay analysis, it is important to understand the historical context. Founded in 1922, the Berlin Institute maintained the principle of only accepting candidates with a medical degree into its training program. This pushed psychoanalysis in the direction of medicalization and challenged the earlier view espoused by both Freud and Ferenczi.

Sandor Rado and Franz Alexander, founders of the psychoanalytic institutes in New York and Chicago, respectively, reinforced the medicalization of psychoanalysis in line with US practice at the time. Abraham Brill, the first psychoanalyst in the US and founder of the New York Psychoanalytic Society, was of the same view, as was Ernst Jones, who was opposed to lay analysis. In a letter to Ferenczi in 1928, Freud wrote:

The inner development of Ψα everywhere runs counter to my intentions, away from lay analysis to the purely medical specialty, which I sense to be ominous for the future of analysis. Actually, I am *only* sure about you that you share my point of view without reservation.

(Freud to Ferenczi, 22 April 1928, 2000, p. 339)

Just as an example, the intensity of the debate around a medical orientation and emigration was palpable at the 42nd APsaA meeting in 1940.[5] Concerning that debate it is interesting to note the different perspectives of two members of the ECRI, Alexander and Rado. Alexander not only underlined the importance of a medical background in psychoanalysis, but also emphasized the difference between the American and European psychoanalysis:

Psychoanalysis in America has developed under circumstances somewhat different from those obtaining in Europe. . . . This difference has expressed itself in the attitude of the American Psychoanalytic Association towards the lay question. The first disagreements between the European and American organizations centered on this very issue (see footnote 4, pp. 32–33) . . . the future of psychoanalysis as a therapeutic method lies in the cooperation and coordination of psychoanalysis with the larger body of medicine.

(ibid., p. 33)

However, he warned of the dangers posed by the European émigrés:

Most of the European psychoanalysts came here in their middle years. They had grown up with a somewhat different emotional and intellectual orientation concerning psychoanalytic practice in its relation to medicine. It was feared that not all of them could easily adopt a new attitude and discard their older convictions and that by creating two opposing orientations a disrupting influence might disturb the development of the powerful but still young American organizations.

(*ibid.*, p. 33)

Jones suggested the following:

[the] two Associations [the IPA and APsaA] should still be united, naturally on equal terms, by adherence to an international body. . . . The Executive of this international body should consist of a President and a secretary, chosen alternatively from America and Europe, and a small Council composed of equal numbers from both Associations.

The main purpose would be:

The organizing of International Congresses to be held every four years, alternatively, in America and Europe according to the residence of the officials. The purpose of such congresses would be simply to effect a personal interchange of scientific knowledge and to discuss any general matters of common interest.

> (Report of the Meeting of the Special Committee on the
> Relation of the American Psychoanalytic Association to
> the International Psychoanalytical Association, p. 31)

It was Rado who made the soberingly realistic recommendation to wait:

> At present, no one knows what the international association consists of. However, we know that while the war is on, no international association can function anyway. When the war will be over and what the world will look like after that . . . no one knows. It does not seem feasible now to provide for action to be taken at some unknown future time, under unknown conditions with regard to an unknown partner.

> (*ibid.*, p. 36)

Practical Matters

There was no question that one had a better chance of being permitted to immigrate if one had a medical degree, but even then one was expected to pass a state medical exam, which, in addition to language issues, was rendered more difficult by the numerous regulations that were particular to each state.

At the same time, the ECRI offered all the help they could to lay analysts, who had two options available to them according to the law at the time: child therapy, which did not qualify as a medical activity, and teaching at state-accredited educational institutions.

Hungarian Analysts and the ECRI[6]

Let's take a closer look at what happened to the Budapest analysts.

A cable was sent from Dr. Pfeiffer of the Hungarian Psychoanalytical Society to the ECRI on April 29, 1941: "Telegraph whether immigration for members [and] candidates[,] some with children over 18[,] possible on superquota [non-quota visa] and also help for [residence permit]. [Potential applicants for] [s]uperquota [non-quota visa] about eight" (Payne Whitney/ Cornell Archives, New York Academy of Medicine, Box 13, p. 48).

The ECRI requested that the National Refugee Office have their representative contact the representative of the Hungarian Psychoanalytic Society while they reviewed their own committee documents.

In April of 1941, the following information was available on the Hungarian analysts. As becomes clear from the figures below, the ECRI provided affidavits for three people, and five of them already had the option of non-quota visas.

Eligible for Non-Quota Visas: 5

Dr. Imre Hermann
Dr. István Hollós
Dr. Zsigmond Pfeiffer
Dr. László Révész
Dr. Lillian Kertész-Rotter

Requiring Affidavits: 12 [*sic!*, 14]

Dr. Renee Amar
Kata Levy
Dr. Margit Dubovitz
Dr. Margit Ormos
Dr. Melchior (Menyhért) Farkashazi
Lilly Perl-Balla
Dr. Miklós Gimes
Zelma Sulamith Rubin Farber
Dr. Lilly Gimes-Hajdu
Dr. Stephen (István) Schönberger
Dr. William (Vilmos) Kapos
Dr. Julius (Gyula) Szuts
Mrs. Imre Major
Dr. Róbert Bak

Have Affidavits Secured by the Committee: 3

Dr. Géza Dukes
Dr. Elizabeth (Erzsébet) Kardos
Dr. Andrew (Endre) Pető

**Psychoanalysts Originally from Hungary (15)
at US Psychoanalytic Societies and Institutes (1925–1942)**

The New York Psychoanalytic Society	The Chicago Institute for Psychoanalysis	The Topeka Institute for Psychoanalysis
Agoston, Tibor	Alexander, Franz	Gero, Georg
Bak, Robert	Benedek, Therese	Rapaport, David
Feldmann, Sandor		Devereux, George
Hann-Kende Fanny		(arrived in 1959)
Lorand, Sandor		
Mahler, Margaret		
Peto, Andrew		
(arrived in 1954)		
Rado, Sandor		
Roheim, Geza		
Spitz, A. René		

Let's look at some more detailed examples.

Exemplary among the heroic efforts of the ECRI is the fact that it wrote over 200 letters in attempting to place David Rapaport – who was a mathematician and psychologist, ergo a lay analyst – until a spot was found for him at Karl Menninger's clinic in Topeka, Kansas. The Menninger Clinic was considered a liberal institution in this conservative Midwestern state. It was practically the only place in the region where European analyst refugees could hope for help. As you all know, Rapaport established a research center at the Menninger Clinic and introduced projective and intelligence tests in clinical practice. In fact, between the 1940s and 1960s, he had such an enormous effect on psychology in the US that diagnostic testing became a very important function among US clinical psychologists.

The ECRI also went to great lengths in aid of Georg Gero. Gero had left Hungary in the first exile and, many years later, he became a member of a group of Marxist analysts surrounding Otto Fenichel in Berlin. He therefore had to leave Germany immediately in 1933. He went to Copenhagen, but Hitler's expansion in Europe included Denmark, with Germany's troops occupying the country in 1940. After this, Gero had to escape a third time. Thanks to the persistent efforts and financial support of Kubie and the ECRI, he and his wife travelled through Sweden, Finland, and the Soviet Union to reach the Pacific Ocean on the Trans-Siberian Express. Gero and his wife trekked around half the globe to reach San Francisco via Japan and finally to New Mexico, where the Committee had arranged a university post for him. One year later, Gero wrote to the Committee in desperation that he was surrounded by nothing but cows in New Mexico, while all his friends – among them, Rado, Annie Reich, Edith Jacobson, and Heinz Hartmann – were in New York. So, the Committee backed his move to New York in 1943. For the rest of Gero's long life, he never set foot outside that city.

Robert Bak also received support from the ECRI in the sum of 200 dollars. In April of 1943, he joined the New York Psychoanalytic Society. In 1944, he became a lecturer at the New York Psychoanalytic Institute. In 1945, he accepted Rado's invitation to become an adjunct professor at Columbia's Psychoanalytic and Psychosomatic Clinic, which Rado had established the year before. In 1947, he became a training analyst and then president of the New York Psychoanalytic Society a decade later (1957–1959). He became a real New Yorker in no time. His elegant office at 985 Fifth Avenue on the Upper East Side proved a memorable spot for both students and patients alike.

The following Hungarian analysts received funding from the ECRI: Dr. Tibor Agoston; Dr. C. Robert Bak; Dr. Sandor Feldmann; Dr. Georg Gero; David Rapaport, PhD; Dr. Fanny von Hann-Kende; and Geza Roheim, PhD.

Financial support for the Hungarians ranged between 200 and 7,900 dollars. On average, they received a few hundred dollars, but an enormous sum had to be paid to aid Gero in his escape and resettlement – almost 8,000 dollars.

Fair Play and Mutuality

Before the Committee brought its work to a close in 1948, it made an appeal to those it had helped to resettle. The Committee asked them to pay back the amount of the support they had received if they were able. The ECRI saw the sum that had been provided as an interest-free loan. According to the ECRI final report, all the Hungarians had paid off their loans and the majority of other applicants who had received aid paid it back. I think beyond the fair play gentlemen's agreement, it had a psychic result, too, as they became free of the often-oppressive burden of long-lasting gratitude.

The ECRI Became an Example to All

After receiving hard news of the Hungarian psychoanalytic community – altogether 17 members and candidates who survived and remained in

Hungary – three originally Hungarian psychoanalysts in New York set up the *Relief Committee for the Hungarian Psychoanalytical Society* in 1945. The committee consisted of Sandor Lorand and Sandor Rado (chairs) and Robert Bak (secretary/treasurer).

Bak wrote a letter to Ernest Kris asking for his help:

> During the past weeks, we have received news from the survivors of the Hungarian Psychoanalytical Society about the terrible losses they have suffered, and about the desolate state they are in at present.
>
> Some members have been killed, some have been deported and have perished in German concentration camps, and some fell in the Battle of Budapest.
>
> The remainder and their families are without adequate food, clothing, and shelter, unable to provide even for their most immediate needs. They have lost almost all their possessions, but not their spirit, and their devotion to our field. They write with great restraint about their miseries, but report that the society meets every fortnight, the research continues, and lectures are being given to the public.
>
> The analysts of Hungarian origin are eager to do the major share, but we need your help, too. We would be very grateful for your generosity, but even your nominal contributions would be of great value to us.
>
> (Mészáros, 2010, p. 610)

The Further Fate of the Émigrés and of Those Who Could not Leave their Countries

Lack of Mourning and the "Fragmented Self"

The question of mourning. For various reasons (political and societal), there was no possibility for mourning either among those who became émigrés in another country or those who survived persecution and remained in their country.

The émigré analysts had to deal with the problem of resettlement and had to try to accommodate new challenges. The necessity of immediate integration into a new country/society works against the mourning process, or at least it delays the mourning of losses of home, language, family, culture – their whole previous life.

A number of American authors, like Robert Prince, have drawn a connection between unprocessed trauma and:

> delayed or incomplete mourning . . . [and the development of] authoritarianism in psychoanalytic institutions . . . as a reliving of the trauma of both fascism and exile, and not merely typical group psychology. Further evidence of the impact of dissociated trauma includes the astonishing scotoma for actual events in the treatment of Holocaust survivors; the extreme privileging of infantile fantasy over reality, and attention to childhood neurosis at the expense of adult catastrophic events.
>
> (Prince, 2009, p. 179)

Emily Kuriloff says, "refugee analysts did not discuss the influence of catastrophe on their work" (Kuriloff, 2014, p. 1). It is an interesting question whether they did so consciously; however, unconsciously, this can be discovered in their theories. Heinz Kohut, who had to leave Vienna in 1938, said in an interview: "I've led two totally different, perhaps unbridgeable lives." As Kohut elaborated: "the problem of the fragmented self" (Kohut cited in Quinn cited in Kuriloff, 2014, p. 2).

"The problem of the fragmented self" appeared among those who remained in Europe, lost their colleagues and friends, and seriously damaged part of their identity and future options because of political reasons. Hungary was liberated and, soon after, occupied by the Soviets, with a new dictatorship formed within several years. Many Jewish survivors believed that the new regime based on communist, leftist values held the promise of a new society without discrimination. In the name of a wrongly interpreted ideology of human equality, the communist regime demanded that the people, and mainly its party members, forsake their earlier identities completely, including religion and ethnicity. Jews who had survived Nazi dictatorship, German invaders, and the country's own collaborators faced another peril: giving up their Jewish identity and "forgetting" everything related to their Jewish background, including their personal traumatic experiences. Whatever the case was – forced emigration or another dictatorial regime – this resulted in an inability to work through traumas, and thus the process of the transgenerational transfer of trauma had begun, both individually and societally.

Common Denominator Among the Soviet Bloc Countries

Beyond all of these, it was the first time in Hungary that *psychoanalysis as a discipline* was persecuted as "the private psychology of imperialism" (Mészáros, 2010, p. 612). To continue psychoanalytic practice became dangerous (Hidas, 1997). This is why the Ferenczi-founded (1913) Hungarian Psychoanalytical Society dissolved itself at the beginning of 1949. Most of the psychoanalysts gave up their practice, with very few of them continuing underground in the face of personal risk. The State Protection Authority (ÁVH) was established in 1950 on the Soviet model of the KGB, with an original aim to seek out war criminals, but very quickly became a power tool to hunt down anyone who challenged the communist regime. The darkest era of Stalinism in Hungary, with a constant fear of arrest and internment, lasted from 1949 till 1953, when Stalin died. The situation eased after his death, followed by uprising in 1956 that was crushed by the Soviet troops. Thousands were arrested, hundreds of thousands emigrated, and a Stalinist dictatorship was changed a lighter version of dictatorial regime after the early 1960s. This process did not leave Hungarian psychoanalysts untouched. Endre Peto, who was the secretary of the Society, lost his first wife just at the end of the war and, soon after it, lost the hope to continue his life as a psychoanalyst. He emigrated after the Hungarian Psychoanalytic Society was dissolved and before the borders of Hungary were closed. A psychoanalyst (István Székács-Schönberger) and a candidate (András József/Adolf Fisch) were politically falsely accused and arrested at the early 1950s.

There were some similarities in the psychoanalysts in the Soviet Bloc countries: personal losses, wounded identity, and the loss of their future psychoanalytic career. As for the common denominator among these countries, the analysts in each group experienced the feeling of loneliness, separation, and enclosure, which led later to a serious deficit of self-esteem.

The societies could not exist anymore, the analytic community became fragmented, and psychoanalysis began its decades of underground and later semi-underground existence. This also damaged the potential for international ties among later generations of psychoanalysts and further decreased individuals' self-esteem. In several studies, Michael Šebek discusses how a totalitarian political system is reflected in the unconscious mind and how it is internalized in the personality, including in the reality principle and development of autonomy (Šebek, 1996). The fragmented, encapsulated traumatic feelings and rejected aggression and hate emerged later in the newly developed life of the psychoanalytic societies in the late 1980s (Mikota and Štajner-Popović, 2005, p. 544).

Closing Remarks

The analysts who were forced to emigrate – many already middle-aged – left behind their culture, their extended families, and their entire lives up to that point to struggle with a new language, to find work immediately, and to integrate into a new society in anticipation of a hopeful future, but unable to mourn their losses. At the same time, the generation in exile spurred on the development of new dimensions in psychoanalysis through cross-pollination and collaboration with their host professional communities. See, for example, ego-psychology and self-psychology, developed in Cincinnati by German-born Heinz Hartmann, Austrian-born Heinz Kohut, and Hungarian-born Paul and Anna Ornstein.

Focusing on the contribution of the émigré Budapest School of psychoanalysts, they influenced the area of psychoanalytic psychosomatics (Balint and Alexander), research on the personality-forming significance of the early mother–child relationship (the Balints, Spitz, Klein, and Mahler), a reinterpretation of the interpersonal dynamic in psychoanalytic therapies (Balint, Benedek), clinical research (Rapaport and Benedek), and the spread of testing methods for use in psychiatric clinics (Rapaport).

In addition, they had a great hand in developing training models and educational structures, and established institutions. Just consider the roles of Sandor Rado and Franz Alexander at their respective psychoanalytic institutes in the US, Michael Balint within the British Psychoanalytical Society, and Clara Lazar Gero, the founder of the Australian Psychoanalytic Society – all of which guaranteed a standard of professional training for the coming generations.

The émigré generation was forced to leave a great deal behind, but perhaps they were compensated for their losses by the experience of being in a more democratic country and joining accepting communities in which they were free to live and work.

When the Emergency Committee was formed, it sensed the historic shift, it changed perspectives, and it prioritized the saving of life. The Committee understood that by helping émigré colleagues settle, they would inevitably change the landscape, the functioning, and the developmental trajectory of US psychoanalytic communities, societies, and institutes. Nonetheless, they chose to express solidarity, created opportunities, disseminated factual information, and asked the émigrés for cooperation and personal responsibility. The Committee was a small NGO: there were very few members, and they asked their peers for support. To solve the problems at hand, they cooperated with organizations that had similar aims and built a network – thus, there came to be very many of them indeed. They achieved the nearly impossible. In only a few years, for as long as it was still possible to cross the ocean, they saved hundreds of European colleagues: psychoanalysts with medical background or lay analysts, social workers, and their families, who exercised an enormous influence on the modernization of psychoanalysis. The story of double exile shows that if hosts and émigrés both work toward overcoming the challenges of integration, the sum of parts will always be greater than the whole.

Notes

1 This paper was prepared based on a lecture at the New School Conference, 2019: *The Émigré Analysts and American Psychoanalysis: History and Contemporary Relevance.*
2 Interview with Sandor Lorand by Lawrence Kolb. Manuscript, 1963. The Library of Congress.
3 This is the original letter (without corrections) from István Hollós to Lawrence S. Kubie, January 9, 1939, *Archives of the British Psycho-Analytical Society* G07/BJ/F01.
4 The pre-story of the Emergency Committee goes back to January with a different name and aims: to maintain the number of émigré experts within certain limits, to direct them to less-preferred professional communities instead of the more popular hubs, and to ensure that psychoanalytic training would continue to remain in the hands of highly qualified and recognized training institutes (Kubie, 1937–1938).
5 The Forty-Second Meeting of the American Psychoanalytic Association. The Netherland Plaza Cincinnati, Ohio, May 19, 20, 21 and 22, 1940. *Bulletin of the American Psychoanalytic Association* 3(1):16–65.
6 This part is based on a reseach that has already been published. See reference: Judit Mészáros, 2010, 2014.

References

Breitman, R., and Kraut, A.M. (1987). *American Refugee Policy and European Jewry, 1933–1945*. Bloomington, IN: Indiana University Press.
Frank, T. (2009). *Double Exile. Migrations of Jewish-Hungarian Professioanals through Germany to the United States, 1919–1945*. Bern: Peter Lang AG, European Academic Publishers.

Brabant, E., Falzeder, E. and Giampieri-Deutsch, P. (Eds.). (2000). *The Correspondence of Sigmund Freud and Sándor Ferenczi*, Volume 3, 1920–1933 trans. P. T. Hoffer. Cambridge, MA: The Belknap Press of Harvard University Press.

Hidas, Gy. (1997). Psychoanalysis in Hungary in the Era of Communism and Postcommunism. *Psychoanalytic Inquiry* 17:486–497.

Jeffrey, W.D. (1989). After the Anschluss. The Emergency Committee on Relief and Immigration of the American Psychoanalytic Association. *The American Psychoanalyst* 2(23):19–37.

Kubie, S. (1939). Letter from Lawrence S. Kubie to István Hollós, 19 January 1939. *Archives of the British Psychoanalytical Society*, G07/BJ/F01/25.

Kuriloff, E.A. (2014). *Contemporary Psychoanalysis and the Legacy of the Third Reich: History, Memory, Tradition.* New York: Routledge.

Kurzweil, E. (1992). Psychoanalytic Science: From Oedipus to Culture. *Psychoanalytic Review* 3(79):341–360.

Mészáros, J. (1998). The Tragic Success of European Psychoanalysis: "The Budapest School." *International Forum of Psychoanalysis* 7:207–214.

Mészáros, J. (2010). Progress and Persecution in the Psychoanalytic Heartland: Antisemitism, Communism and the Fate of Hungarian Psychoanalysis. *Psychoanalytic Dialogues* 20(5):600–622.

Mészáros, J. (2012). Effect of Dictatorial Regimes on the Psychoanalytic Movement in Hungary Before and After World War II. In J. Damousi and M.B. Plotkin (Eds.), *Psychoanalysis and Politics. History of Psychoanalysis Under Conditions of Restricted Political Freedom* (pp. 79–108). New York: Oxford University Press.

Mészáros, J. (2014). *Ferenczi and Beyond: Exile of the Budapest School and Solidarity in the Psychoanalytic Movement During the Nazi Years.* London: Karnac Books.

Mikota, V., and Štajner-Popović, T. (2005). Developing Psychoanalysis Under Socio-Political Pressure: Viewpoints from Eastern Europe. *The International Journal of Psychoanalysis* 86(2):543–546.

Prince, R. (2009). Psychoanalysis Traumatized: The Legacy of the Holocaust. *The American Journal of Psychoanalysis* 69(3):179–194.

Šebek, M. (1996). The Fate of the Totalitarian Object. *International Forum of Psychoanalysis* (Vol. 5, No. 4, pp. 289–294).

Thompson, N.L. (2012). The Transformation of Psychoanalysis in America: The transformation of Psychoanalysis in America: Émigré Analysts and the New York Psychoanalytic Society and Institute, 1935–1961. *Journal of the American Psychoanalytic Association* 60:9–44.

(1940). The Forty-Second Meeting of The American Psychoanalytic Association the Netherland Plaza Cincinnati, Ohio May 19, 20, 21 and 22, 1940. *Bulletin of the American Psychoanalytic Association* 3(1):16–65.

Help, Health, Husbands, and Hutzpah

The Lives of Five Women Analysts

Klara Naszkowska

> *Reportedly, when asked how she survived, Marianne Kris said: "You need the three H's. You need good help, good health, and a good husband,"*
> *to which Jenny Waelder-Hall replied: "There's a fourth H. . . . Hutzpah."*
>   (Malkin, Dec. 14, 2000, p. 54)

Introduction

This paper examines the personal and professional biographies of five remarkable Jewish women: Grete Bibring, Helene Deutsch, Dora Hartmann, Marianne Kris, and Jenny Waelder-Hall, each of them at the core of the prewar psychoanalytic movement in Europe. In the progressive, social democratic Red Vienna of the 1920s and early 1930s, these women (and their husbands) formed a close-knit circle of friends that met regularly every Saturday evening to talk, play cards and dine together. Like all early Freudians, they were not "just" medically trained analysts or future analysts, but also cosmopolitan intellectuals who were extremely well-versed in European high culture. Every Saturday, they would indulge in an "exchange of clinical experience [that] went on day and night," "a constant interchange of ideas" and heated intellectual debates on cultural, social and political issues (Hartmann, January 31, 1973, p. 25).

When the rise of Engelbert Dollfuss' Christian Austro-Fascism in 1933–34 snuffed out social democracy, psychoanalysis lost its cultural, educational and intellectual ground in Austria. On top of that, Dollfuss and his successor, Kurt Schuschnigg, introduced over four hundred anti-semitic decrees and regulations between 1933 and the beginning of war in 1939 that virtually stripped Austrian Jews of their citizenship rights and properties. Regardless of the dire and still worsening political and social

DOI: 10.4324/9781003266228-6

situation they found themselves in, Vienna-based psychoanalysts tended to remain in Austria until the country was officially annexed to the Third Reich on March 13, 1938. Until the Anschluss became a reality, they had been inclined to mistakenly believe (often due to dissociation) that Austria was relatively safe for them and beyond Hitler's reach. Almost all of them belonged to a generation of fully assimilated Jewish intellectuals, immersed in the culture of the German-language world. They identified as Austrians and, thus, did not perceive themselves as potential victims of Nazi persecution. Also, they deluded themselves in believing that Germans and Austrians, responsible for creating art, philosophy and literature they admired, were incapable of such brutality. They blamed the antisemitic violence and Nazi persecution taking place in Germany since 1933 on the rabble. Additionally, Sigmund Freud, Anna Freud and the then-president of the International Psychoanalytic Association, Ernest Jones (1932–49), strongly encouraged them to remain in Vienna as long as possible to secure the future of the psychoanalytic movement and its institutions.

As a result, out of the group of five women under study, only Helene Deutsch left Europe before the Anschluss, on September 13, 1935 (Ellis Island Passenger Records). She was leaving a fascist and deeply antisemitic Austria behind, but she was not escaping persecution. Instead, Helene Deutsch was searching for new professional opportunities for herself and caring for her son, Martin. The circumstances of the departures of the remaining four women and their husbands from Vienna were entirely different. They all fled Nazi-occupied Vienna in haste, as soon as they could – Jenny Waelder-Hall directly to the US with Helene Deutsch's help, Grete Bibring and Marianne Kris to London, Dora Hartmann to Paris.

After eventually reaching America, all five women analysts became decisive in shaping the development of Freudian theory and practice in the US. Their contributions notwithstanding, are now neglected and at risk of being forgotten.[1] The aim of the paper is to reclaim and reconstruct their life stories and complex multiple identities as the ceiling-shattering New Women, Jews, pioneers in psychoanalysis, refugees, German-speaking emigrants, New Yorkers, mothers and more by utilizing the methodology of a cultural, social and personal historian. Gaps in present knowledge about the five women will be bridged with information from two types of sources: historical documents and documents of personal history. By bringing oral histories to attention – an approach that remains quite new and underexplored – I intend to permit these women's voices to be heard.

The Black Cat Group in Vienna

The bunch, consisting of Helene and Felix Deutsch, Grete and Edward Bibring, Dora and Heinz Hartmann, Marianne and Ernst Kris, and Jenny Waelder-Hall and Robert Waelder started meeting each Saturday evening sometime in mid-1920s and continued until Helene Deutsch's emigration in September of 1935.[2] They called themselves the Black Cat group after the card game *Die schwarze Katze*, a variant of whist. However, any card playing was just a pretext. The group met to discuss psychoanalytic developments, patient cases and broader cultural issues.

They meetings were usually hosted by "Hala" Deutsch, as her friends called her, and her husband, Felix, who lived in a gorgeous nineteenth-century apartment house at Wollzeile 33 in the dead center of Vienna (in the first district of the inner city, Germ. *Innere Stadt*). In April of 1945, during the Fall of Berlin when the Russian Red Army took the city from Germany sometime around Hitler's birthday and shortly before his suicide, a shell hit the roof of the apartment house, but the building survived. The Black Cat group occasionally met at other members' homes but, according to Jenny Waelder-Hall, they all preferred to meet at the Deutsches, who had an excellent cook: "Hala liked us in her house and she had a very wonderful cook so it was nothing but a gastronomic delight to spend the evening there;" "we had a very lovely time there every Saturday" (Waelder-Hall, August 1973, p. 6).

It is also worth pointing out that, at that time, in the mid-1920s and early 1930s, Helene Deutsch was already a recognized and well-respected analyst of international stature, holding a significant position within the Vienna Psychoanalytic Society (WPV). Born in 1884, she was the group's only woman representing the first generation of psychoanalysts, defined as born in the 1870s and 1880s. The others were of the second generation, defined as born from the turn of the century to the 1910s: Jenny Waelder-Hall in 1898, Grete Bibring in 1899, Marianne Kris in 1900 and Dora Hartmann in 1902. Hence, Helene Deutsch was about fifteen years older than the other women in the Black Cat group. When, in January 1925, she was appointed the first director of the newly opened Vienna Training Institute, Grete Bibring had only just qualified as a doctor and started seeing analysands the year prior and then, in 1925, was officially accepted as an associate member of WPV,[3] while Dora Hartmann, Marianne Kris, and Jenny Waelder-Hall were all still in medical school until they graduated later in 1925.

Many younger analysts considered Helene Deutsch to be a domineering "titan" representing the orthodox establishment of the psychoanalytic movement in Vienna and beyond, and a decisive influence on their lives.[4] When asked where they met, Jenny Waelder-Hall initially replies: "we met at Hala Deutsch," and only then corrects herself, "at the Deutsches" (Waelder-Hall, August 1973, p. 6). On the other hand, Helene Deutsch saw herself as a representative of the younger, more liberal generation of psychoanalysts. According to her, the Black Cat group was "the natural impulse of the young to create their own psychological atmosphere in contrast to the conservative older generation" (Deutsch, 1973a, p. 167).

Who Were the Jewish New Women

When it comes to ethnical, familial and religious backgrounds, the Black Cat women were model New Women. The origins of the term can be traced back to Sarah Grand (née Frances Elizabeth Clark, 1854–1943), an Irish-born suffragette and feminist author of "New Woman" novels and of the 1894 essay "The New Aspects of the Woman Question," where she used the phrase "new woman" as an aside (Grand, 1894; Bonnell, 1995). She described her as beyond men's comprehension, "a little above" them, "sitting apart in silent contemplation all these years, thinking and thinking, until at last she solved the problem and proclaimed for herself what was wrong with Home-is-the-Woman's-Sphere, and prescribed the remedy" (Grand, 1894, p. 271). The literary heroines of the *fin-de-siècle* years were then projected onto real-life women. Today, in the context of social and cultural history, the phrase New Women refers to "university women of the early twentieth century, who defied conventional expectations . . . by seeking personal self-fulfillment through higher education and careers in traditionally male professional fields" (Freidenreich, 2002, p. xvii).

Typically for the New Women, all five Black Cat women were Jews by birth; both parents of each were Jewish. Consistently, they came from culturally and socially assimilated, wealthy, middle- to upper-class families. Their parents were either nonobservant or only observed some Jewish holidays, as so-called Silky Jews (adopted from a *bekishe*, the black-silk coat worn on Shabbos, Jewish holidays and other special events).

Due to a combination of cultural, social, legal and personal reasons, most mothers of professional women in the early decades of the twentieth century had no university education and were homemakers, while their fathers and other male family members were cultured professionals, typically doctors, lawyers or businessmen, often well-known and respected by their local Jewish communities. New Women often identified with their better-educated, more liberal fathers and tended to distance themselves or flatly reject their mothers' more conventional, even Victorian values. They often had close relationships with their fathers, engaged in leisure activities together and relentlessly pursued professional careers in male-dominated areas, commonly choosing the same occupation as their fathers, especially in the case of physicians. Regarding Black Cat women, all of whom were medical doctors, two fathers were lawyers, two were businessmen and one was a renowned pediatrician, while all mothers were homemakers.

It is typically much more difficult to unearth information about mothers of the first women psychoanalysts than fathers. Psychoanalysts and other mental health professionals who conducted interviews as part of various oral history projects in the late 1960s to 1990s extremely rarely ask any personal questions that are of interest to a cultural historian. In the interviews conducted by family members – typically children and grandchildren of the women under study – the interviewees themselves tend to focus on their professional biographies. When pushed by the next generations, nostalgic for information about their family roots, they usually focus on their fathers.

A large contingent of the first women psychoanalysts were born in then-occupied Poland. Two of the Black Cat women, Helene Deutsch and Jenny Waelder-Hall, came from Galicia, a multicultural, multinational region of the Polish-Lithuanian Commonwealth that had been created in 1772 during the First Partition of Poland when it was annexed the Hapsburg Empire (Austrian Empire from 1804; Austro–Hungarian Empire from 1867), and ceased to exist with the end of World War I, when it was divided between Poland and Ukraine in 1918. At their birth, the identities of these women already consisted of four components: Jewish, Galician, Polish and Austrian (see Wolff, 2010 on the subject of Galician identity).

Helene Deutsch (née Rosenbach) was born on October 9, 1884, in a mid-size town of Premissel (Przemyśl in present-day Poland). For her, who went on to study, work and live in Vienna, and then in Boston, Przemyśl remained a "real home" (Deutsch, 1973a, p. 175). When she was growing up, the town was almost 40 percent Jewish. Her father, Wilhelm Rosenbach (1844/5–1919), a prominent criminal lawyer and a scholar of international law, was an important figure in the town's Jewish community. Their house, located at Rynek 26 in the very center of the town, "was a microcosm of the Polish-Jewish society of Przemyśl at that time" (21). Rosenbach was the first Jew to be appointed as a juridical representative of Galicia to the Federal Court in Vienna and he was held in high regard in Przemyśl and beyond. According to her own words, Helene Deutsch strongly identified with her father as his intellectual heir. She repeatedly stated in her memoir and interviews: "I was his boy" (Deutsch March 28, 1973c).

Helene Deutsch devoted chapter IV of her memoir from 1973 to her mother, Regina (née Fass, 1854–1941), after Przemyśl, her father and her sisters. Regina Rosenbach came from a well-to-do family of fabric shop owners. She was briefly in a boarding school in Switzerland, as many girls from good families were. Helene Deutsch called her an aggressive, "imposing individual" who "ruled [the] model household like a despot, from a throne situated in a niche off the dining room" (Deutsch, 1973a, p. 63) and repeatedly stated that she "hated" her mother.

Her compatriot Jenny Waelder-Hall (née Pollak) was born on November 16, 1898, in Lemberg (Lviv in present-day Ukraine), the capital of Galicia, and a cultural and academic center of East-Central Europe of long standing. In the 1920s and 1930s, as Lwów in independent Poland, it would be home to the country's third-largest Jewish community, numbering some 110,000 (Spector and Wigoder, 2001, pp. 769–775, 1033–1035). Jenny's father, Jacob (Jakób) Pollak (1867–1929), was a businessman engaged in international trade with neighboring countries, "a very elegant [man] with little black ebony cane with a silver handle" (Husek June 8, 1995, p. 74). His father had been a well-educated "gentlemen farmer" who owned the village of Rozsniów (in present-day Ukraine) (6–7).[5] It had been Jacob Pollak's intention to study law, but he was forced by tuberculosis to end his education in gymnasium. Law was a hobby and he often assisted friends, arbitrating in business cases. Jenny Waelder-Hall's mother, Amalia Marjem Malke (née Rosenberg, 1864–1932), was born in Lemberg to a religious family in which both Old and New Testaments were read. Her father, Rafael Rosenberg, was a merchant.

Jenny Waelder-Hall's family home was bilingual, Polish and German (Husek, 1995, p. 2; Husek, 1996). When the Russian military defeated the Austro-Hungarians in the Battles of Lemberg at the start of the First World War (August 23–September 12, 1914), fifteen-year-old Jenny Waelder-Hall experienced forced emigration for the first time. Her family had to flee Russian-occupied Poland for Vienna. They arrived there as refugees, "stacked like cattle into . . . trains" (2). From then until her second emigration to America in 1938, Jenny Waelder-Hall lived in Vienna.

Grete Bibring (née Margarethe Lehner) was born in Vienna on January 11, 1899, in a very wealthy intellectual-bourgeoise family. Her father, Moritz Lehner (1864–1936), was a Viennese "business man but . . . very intellectual" (G. Bibring April 13, 1976, p. 22), "extremely well read . . . a freethinker and Social Democrat" (Gifford, n.d., p. 1). He had attended gymnasium, but after the Panic of 1873 provoked a financial crisis in Vienna, he was forced to drop out and find work. When Grete was little, he owned a factory that produced margarine and synthetic cooking oils that played a significant role during the food shortages of the First World War. His younger brother, Oskar Lehner (1868–1937), was the general manager of what was then the most luxurious hotel in Vienna, the Imperial, built in 1863–1866 as the Duke of Württemberg's palace and converted into a hotel in 1873. In the 1930s, the hotel was co-owned by a Jewish businessman from Brno, Samuel Schallinger (1867–1943), who was later forced by the Nazis to sell his share before being deported to Theresienstadt concentration camp and murdered (National Archives, Prague; Terezín Initiative Institut). Everyone who was someone stayed in the Hotel Imperial: state leaders, politicians, artists. The celebration of Sigmund Freud's eightieth birthday was hosted there on May 8, 1936. Almost two years later, Hitler stayed in the hotel following the Anschluss of March 13, 1938, and famously ordered a bunker to be built underneath.

Grete Bibring's mother, Victoria Josephine (née Stengel, 1868–?), also came from Vienna (Jewishgen). She "brought [her daughter] up very – in a very Victorian spirit. [And was] sex-rejecting" (Bibring April 17, 1976, p. 8) and was a homemaker.

Dora Hartmann (née Karplus) was born in Vienna on June 16, 1902. She had a very close relationship with her father, Sigmund Karplus (1861–1928), a doctor of law, originally from the village of Horní Moštěnice, then in Austro-Hungary (present-day Czech Republic). They were both adventurous mountaineers and naturalists with shared passions. He encouraged her to climb the summits of the glaciated massif Piz Palü (possibly the first woman to do so). Her mother, Ludmilla (née Kaufmann) (1866–1940s), was formal, old-fashioned and dignified.

Marianne Kris (née Rie) was also born in Vienna, on May 27, 1900. Her father, Oskar Rie (1863–1931), was a well-known and highly respected Viennese pediatrician. He was also a very close friend of Sigmund Freud's, assisting him in neurological research in the 1890s, an early member of the Vienna Psychoanalytic Society (beginning in 1908), a pediatrician to his children and "Otto" in Freud's famous "Irma's injection" dream (Freud [1900] 2010). Marianne Kris's mother, Melanie Rie (?–1930) (née Bondy), was a very well-off granddaughter of a sugar-factory owner and, according to her grandson, Anton "Tony" Kris, "an obsessional *hausfrau*" (A. Kris, personal communication, Dec. 27, 2020). While Marianne Kris is not on record about rejecting her mother's lifestyle and values, she is barely mentioned in the three lengthy interviews conducted in the 1970s. Marianne Kris did, however, call her mother "a very gifted and an eager painter" (M. Kris July 25, 1973, pp. 1–2) and, not without hurdle, managed to bring some of her paintings with her to London and then to New York.

Education Instead of a Dowry

Naturally, Helene Deutsch had wanted to follow her father into law, but that was simply not an option at the time: women were not allowed to study law in the Austro-Hungarian Empire. By the time law schools in Austria and the newly independent Poland opened its doors to women in 1919, Helene Deutsch was already a practicing psychoanalyst with a degree in psychiatry.

Since law was unavailable to her, Helene Deutsch chose medicine. Medical schools in the Austro-Hungarian Empire started accepting women in 1900.[6] The first woman to practice medicine in the Austro-Hungarian Empire, Gabriele Possanner von Ehrenthal (1860–1940), took her medical degree from the University of Zurich in 1893 and then received a license to practice in Austria. Switzerland had been the second country in Europe to admit female students, after England, and for three decades was the only German-speaking country to do so. First to open its doors to women in 1864 was the University of Zurich; the universities in Geneva and Bern swiftly followed its lead. Until German and Austrian academic institutions began admitting women, Swiss universities absorbed a great influx of foreign women students. During that period, over 90 percent of their female students were immigrants, mainly from Eastern Europe (Holmes, 1984).

Jewish women immediately came to make up a very high proportion of medical students. Of the first eighteen women receiving medical degrees in Vienna by 1906, two-thirds were Jews. Jewish women would comprise almost 40 percent of the female students at the University of Vienna medical school by the early 1930s (Friedenreich, 1996, p. 80).

The preponderance of Jewish women among medical students in the first years of the twentieth century came about due to a combination of socio-economic and cultural factors. Since they, in large part, came from wealthy families, their parents did not have to worry about their daughters needing to marry into wealth and could afford to educate them well. Typically, their fathers had received some form of college-level education and valued the benefits of higher education. They provided their daughters with financial as well as moral support to pursue university educations and professional careers (see: Friedenreich, 2002). In Jewish Orthodox families there was also a custom that women combined household duties with professional work, however, and helped support the family financially. In part, the arrangement allowed men to dedicate more time to the study of the Talmud. Daughters of Orthodox Jews typically pursued university education in professions viewed as practical, including medicine and law.

Helene Deutsch, a representative of the first generation of analysts, did not have her parents' support to go to university and decided to do so against their wishes. Her mother, Regina, believed that "a girl from a good family does not go to university" (Deutsch March 28, 1973c) and "strenuous[ly] . . . oppos[ed]" her daughter's plan to study medicine. Helene Deutsch reports that she rebelled against her: "My mother had no influence on my education, and her contribution to my intellectual values only existed in a negative sense: I reacted against hers" (Deutsch, 1973a, pp. 68, 66). However, even her idealized, better-educated and much more liberal father opposed Helene Deutsch's idea to pursue a university education. Both her parents expected her to bring her education to an end at the age of fourteen when she graduated from a private primary school for girls in Przemyśl (a *Lyzeum*) run by Zofia Iwanicka and marry in the near future.

Another obstacle on her path to an advanced education was that Helene Deutsch completed said *Lyzeum* instead of an eight-year-long secondary school called a gymnasium, which provided a comprehensive classical and scientific college-level curriculum. At that time, a gymnasium was the sole institution in Europe preparing students for university education, and almost the exclusive path to enrollment. The classical and scientific course load included eight grades of Latin, which was essential for medical school, as well as Greek, history, natural sciences, physics and mathematics (Bibring March 23, 1975). Gymnasium studies concluded at the age of seventeen or eighteen with a rigorous final written and oral exam called *Matura* in the Austro-Hungarian Empire.

Regardless of said impediments, Helene Deutsch was determined to continue her education. She came up with an extremely ambitious and fearless plan. She threatened to leave home if her father did not sign a contract supporting her plan to take the *Matura* on her own, assisted by hired tutors. He agreed, and it took her about five years to pass the exam. Then she passed the university entrance exam in Krakau (Kraków in present-day Poland) in February of 1907, which was required for non-gymnasium candidates. As a woman, she had to receive special permission to take it (Deutsch, 1973a, pp. 30–47). In 1907, she enrolled in the famous medical school at the University of Vienna, founded in 1365 as the Medical Faculty of the Alma Mater Rudolfina, as one of seven glass ceiling-shattering women in her class of five to six hundred students; three of them would graduate (Deutsch, 1973a, p. 94). In the early twentieth century, it was the second largest medical school in German-speaking countries and one of the leading medical schools in the world – until its faculty became infested with racism, eugenics, and antisemitism in late 1920s and 1930s, many years before Hitler's march on Austria in March of 1938.

While the Black Cat women were studying in Vienna, Austrian universities were prone to antisemitic bias, pressures and violence. Politicized antisemitism increased markedly in the Austro-Hungarian Empire from the 1880s. The Christian Social Party, the major conservative political party established in 1891, won an absolute majority in municipal elections in the capital in 1895. Its populist leader, Karl Lueger, became the mayor of Vienna in 1897 (serving until his death in 1910) and led what was the largest antisemitic movement in Europe.[7] The Christian Social Party combined religious, cultural, and economic antisemitism and "blamed" the secularization and modernization of Austrian people, capitalism and liberalism on Jewish influences (Pauley, 1992).

One of male students in Helene Deutsch's class was Eduard Pernkopf (1888–1955), an ardent Nazi, member of NSDAP since 1933, member of the SA (*Sturmabteilung*) paramilitary wing (the Nazi Brownshirts) since

1934, and an avid proponent of Nazi eugenics, racial hygiene and the compulsory mass sterilization implemented under Germany's 1933 Law for the Prevention of Hereditary Diseased Offspring. Already as a student, Pernkopf was politically active as a member of the nationalistic organization, Die Akademische Burschenschaft Allemania (Student Academic Fraternity of Germany). In the 1930s, during the relentless process of "Nazification" and "DeJudification" of Austro-German medicine, a field then prevalently Jewish, many "non-Aryan" physicians were replaced by political appointees adhering to National Socialist principles of Nazi eugenics, racial hygiene and the compulsory mass sterilization (Zeidman, 2020). Following the Anschluss of March 13, 1938, the "cleansing" of medical Faculty in Vienna was a "remarkably smooth and quick running . . . operation" with "little opposition [being] voiced by colleagues remaining in the Faculty" (Ernst, 1995, p. 750). Three days after the annexation, Pernkopf became dean of the medical school. Under his deanship, 153 of the 197 members of medical faculty were dismissed (almost 78%) within just a few days of the Anschluss. All remaining professors had to submit proof of their "Aryan" descent – their parents' birth certificates and those of their spouses. If they passed a review, they "had to give an oath of loyalty to Hitler" (750). In 1943, Pernkopf was named the president of the University of Vienna.

Nonetheless, the Black Cat women did not talk about experiencing antisemitism as medical students in Vienna. Helene Deutsch went as far to claim: "I was born in antisemitic Poland and grew up in Vienna during its most intense antisemitic phase, but it was only in America that I encountered personal antisemitism for the first time" (Deutsch, 1973a, p. 188).

Helene Deutsch did recall facing gender discrimination at the university. She was called "Mr. Deutsch" by one professor of internal medicine, Franz Chvostek Jr. (1864–1944), who refused to conduct exams for women and was shocked by her extensive knowledge (Deutsch, n.d., p. 32). Chvostek was known to be a determined opponent of women's studies, a nationalist and antisemite. "Under [him], this clinic became known as a hotbed for Pan-German nationalist and Nazi agitation" (Czech, 2018). In 1955, the Chvostekgasse at the very edge of Vienna was renamed after him (from Feldgasse) (Rathkolb, Autengruber, Nemec, and Wenninger, 2013).

Helene Deutsch took her degree in psychiatry in 1912 or 1913 (Deutsch, 1973a, p. 107; Roazen, 1985, p. 97).

The remaining Black Cat women also studied at and graduated from the medical school in Vienna but their paths to education were much simpler for the four second-generation analysts than they were for Helene Deutsch. Most importantly, differently from Regina and Wilhelm Rosenbach, the parents of Grete Bibring, Dora Hartmann, Jenny Waelder-Hall and Marianne Kris all supported their daughters' decision to pursue a university education, to various degrees. As a result of their parents' endorsement, each of the second-generation women graduated from a gymnasium with a diploma that allowed them to enroll in medical school without having to study with private tutors and take additional exams – obstructions that Helene Deutsch had to overcome. Apart from having their parents' financial and moral support, they enjoyed a much more liberal atmosphere of the progressive, social democratic Red Vienna. When they reached the age of matriculation shortly after World War I, the Hapsburg Empire was no more and the world was buzzing with change that affected women's rights.

It can be gleaned from her interviews that Grete Bibring was absolutely free to decide about her education. After receiving a primary education and learning foreign languages at home from governesses and tutors, she enrolled in a girls' gymnasium in Vienna. She vividly describes the rigid academic atmosphere of her school:

> I went to school in the morning, we stayed in school until 1, I think, then I went home and I worked and prepared until about 10 in the evening, day after day after day. . . . So, we were really scholars. It had a medieval touch. . . . [W]e never, never, never over 8 years talked about a boy. . . . Never. Never. We were much more discreet about it.
>
> (Bibring April 17, 1976, pp. 5–6)

Before settling for medicine, she had considered becoming a classicist, botanist and chemist. Finally, after graduating from the gymnasium at the age of nineteen in 1918, Grete Bibring enrolled in a medical school. She stated: "I always went my own way. I was a little bit of a maverick without knowing it" (17). Even her very conservative mother did not question her daughter's choices. She did make one objection, after Grete had already matriculated. Victoria Lehler did not want her daughter to spend time in a study room with men. Grete responded by marrying one of her colleagues, Edward, at the age of twenty-two in December 1921.

Grete Bibring reported on gender discrimination similar to that directed at Helene Deutsch. She recalled having an exam stretched out "all day long" by another professor who resented grading her with "an excellent" score because she was a woman (Bibring April 11, 1976, p. 22). She took her degree in psychiatry in 1924.

It comes as no surprise that all three daughters of Jakob and Amalia Pollak – Jenny Waelder-Hall, Bettina and Helen – took university degrees and had distinguished careers. Their father was very vocal on the issues of their education. He reportedly said to them: "Listen, kids. You won't get any dowry, but you will get an education" (Husek, 1995, p. 81). Their mother, Amalia, did not oppose her daughters' decision to pursue university education. An added motivation to study for all three sisters may have been the difficult situation their mother found herself in as a non-earner when she and her husband separated for a period. That demonstrated to their daughter(s) the value of financial independence from men (von Hippel, personal communication, January 25, 2021).

Jenny Waelder-Hall began her education at a German school that had been established by her grandfather's brother in Lemberg (Husek, 1995, p. 2). She then attended the excellent private girls gymnasium, opened and directed by Jozefa S. Goldblatt-Kamerling in 1899 where 99 percent of students were Jewish (Bilewicz, 1997, p. 63). After her family had fled the city when the Russian military defeated the Austro-Hungarians in the Battle of Lemberg in 1914, she continued her education at a girls' gymnasium in Vienna established and run by her older sister, Bettina. Bettina, known as Betke (1891–1960; later Bettina Neuer, Tagger, then Bruckner), had received her PhD in history from the University of Vienna shortly before the First World War. She then founded three secondary schools for Polish refugees in Vienna, one each for girls and boys and one a vocational school.

After graduation from the gymnasium, Jenny Waelder-Hall entered the medical school in Vienna in 1919, at the age of twenty, and graduated in 1925 with a specialization in pediatrics. At the university, she met Grete Bibring, who sparked her interest in psychoanalysis. Jenny Waelder-Hall's younger sister, Helen (later Helen Husek), born in 1903 in Stanislau, received a PhD in chemistry from the University of Vienna in 1928.

Dora Hartmann received a primary education at home, then graduated from a Viennese gymnasium with a *Matura* and enrolled in a medical school without any hurdles. She enjoyed the full moral and financial backing of her family to do so. Her father, with whom she was close, thought that women could not survive the rigours of medical school but didn't stop her from becoming a doctor (L. Hartmann, personal communication, January 8, 2021). Her mother was less vocal about it, but she herself had wanted to become a doctor. When Austrian medical schools finally admitted female students in 1900, however, Ludmilla was already thirty-four and had three small children. Dora Hartmann suggested that her career decision might have been informed by her mother's unfulfilled dream. Her interest in medicine may have been additionally sparked by her two uncles, both highly acclaimed doctors. Her father's brother, Johann Paul Karplus (1866–1936), was a neurologist and psychiatrist. One of the streets in Vienna, Karplusgasse, was named in his honor. Her maternal uncle, professor Rudolf Kaufmann (1871–1927), was chief physician at the polyclinic in Vienna and head of the cardiology department. She said: "[T]hat was an old idea of mine. I was not even ten years old when I decided I will become a doctor and I will become a doctor who works with children" (D. Hartmann January 31, 1973, p. 1). Dora Hartmann took her degree in medicine in 1925, the same year as Jenny Waelder-Hall, also with a specialization in pediatrics.

Like the other Viennese Black Cats, Marianne Kris also received her primary education from private tutors. She then wanted to study in gymnasium, like her future friends, but her family didn't regard her as "terribly intelligent" (M. Kris July 25, 1973, p. 4) and worried about her alleged heart condition. She was allowed to attend a *Lyzeum*, a girls' school that required considerably less work where students were "prepared for a nice housewife existence" (6). She repeatedly asked her father for a transfer to gymnasium and, at fourteen, he finally allowed one. Marianne Kris's strong identification with her father, that she was fully aware of, prompted her to follow in his footsteps into pediatrics. She said, I was:

absolutely sure from eight years on [that I wanted to be a pediatrician] and not waver for a moment from that time on.... [A]fter all, I was obviously very much identified with my father and wanted to go into medicine.

(M. Kris July 25, 1973, p. 7)

As I have already mentioned, when interviewed, Marianne Kris did not spend much time on her mother, Melanie Rie. At the same time, in her brief description of her mother as "very related to other people," "fair [and] very attentive" (7–8) and a confidante to many, Melanie comes across as a proto-analyst (to my knowledge, a connection unrecognized by Marianne Kris). It also seems that Marianne Kris inherited the qualities of a great analyst from her mother. Marianne Kris's children, Anna and Anton "Tony," describe her as trusted by everyone, "universally loved" and "universally appreciated" (A. Kris, personal communication, Dec. 27, 2020; Kris Wolff, January 21, 2018, p. 5), echoing Marianne's portrayal of Melanie.

After graduating from the gymnasium, Marianne Kris enrolled in the medical school and took her degree in pediatrics in 1925, the same year as Jenny Waelder-Hall and Dora Hartmann. To the best of my knowledge, none of these three women ever mentioned experiencing gender discrimination or antisemitism as students.

Freud and Politics

The year Helene Deutsch enrolled in medical school (in 1907) was when she first read Freud's writings. She first attended meetings of the Vienna Psychoanalytic Society (WPV) during the war years and was elected to full membership in 1918 (Nunberg and Federn, 1975, pp. 296, 310). In August of that year, she began about a year-long analysis with Freud. She was most probably considered a "mild case," so she came only three days a week for one-hour sessions instead of the customary six hours per week. The main goal of her analysis was to train her (May, 2008, p. 85). Freud's decision to break the analysis before it was rendered complete must have hurt Helene Deutsch. On the other hand, despite being brief and incomplete, the training analysis with "the professor" secured her position within both the Vienna group and the International Psychoanalytic Association (IPA) (Deutsch, 1973a, p. 133; May, 2008, p. 85). Most importantly, in 1924, the year she turned forty, she was appointed the first director of the Vienna Training Institute.[8]

In preparation for her new role, Helene Deutsch traveled to Berlin to observe the organization of the first psychoanalytic training institute, the Berlin Psychoanalytic Polyclinic, opened in 1920 with Max Eitingon as president. The institute in Vienna was to be modelled on it. With the collapse of the Austro-Hungarian Empire in 1918 and setting of new boundaries of Czechoslovakia, Hungary, Poland, Romania and Yugoslavia (initially Kingdom of Serbs, Croats and Slovenes), where 90% of the population of the former empire now lived, the Austrian population was reduced to

7 million and the country lost its position as the cultural and political center of the German-speaking world. At the same time, Germany kept most of its territory and population of around 60 million after World War I. Hence, with Freud's blessing, the first training institute was opened in Berlin and, for the next thirteen years, the city became the heart of the psychoanalytic movement. Vienna retook its central position in 1933 after Hitler was named chancellor of Germany and almost all Berlin-based analysts fled the country, including to Austria.

The so-called Eitingon model of the Berlin Psychoanalytic Polyclinic that was to be implemented in Vienna had a tripartite structure. According to it, an institute was to provide three services: training of candidates, research facilities and treatment of patients. The training program had three parts as well: personal/training analysis, supervised cases, and seminars and discussion groups.

Grete Bibring first read Freud independently in 1916. She was only seventeen at that time and in seventh grade of the gymnasium. She remembered it the following way:

[I]n psychology class . . . one of the students got up and told us that her father, a physician in Vienna, had played cards with a friend, Dr. Freud, every Saturday, and Freud told him and the other men in the group that academic psychology figured out some very important parts of what is going on psychologically in people and what motivates them, and what influences their lives, though they are not aware of it. And he called these factors unconscious factors.

The information about the unconscious made Grete Bibring "very curious," so, on her way home, she stopped at a bookstore and picked up one of Freud's books, *Wit and its Relationship to the Unconscious*. She:

did not like it at all. It was confusing; it wasn't very interesting but [she] didn't give up. [She] went back and asked for another book, [*The Psychopathology of Everyday Life*]. Now, that was very different – thought provoking – it was very interesting.

(Bibring March 23, 1975)

Two years and many Freud's books later in 1918, in her first year of medical school, she set up a Vienna Seminar for Sexology with five fellow students, including three future analysts: Otto Fenichel, Edward Bibring and Wilhelm Reich.[9] The initiative came from Fenichel. He passed around a note inviting medical students interested in subjects that were – according to him – taught insufficiently or not addressed at all, to meet after lectures. Grete Bibring immediately decided to join Fenichel and encouraged her two close colleagues, Edward Bibring and Wilhelm Reich, to do so.

The group started with endocrinology, but soon focused entirely on sexology and psychoanalysis. The Vienna Seminar for Sexology could have been the study group Grete Bibring's mother was so worried about. Taking advantage of Freud's custom to reserve a couple hours each afternoon for patients without appointments, the group approached him and "asked simply 'What does that mean?' [about his ideas] 'What does he advise [they] should read after it?' And sometimes . . . simply debated [him]" (Bibring March 23, 1975). Freud gladly addressed all of the issues they raised and invited them to join the WPV as guests (Bibring March 23, 1975). At that time, there was no training institute in Vienna; future analysts "trained" in a very informal way by attending meetings of the WPV and lectures. The same year that the decision was made to set up the Vienna Institute and Helene Deutsch was named its director, 1924, Grete Bibring qualified as a doctor and, a mere day later, started seeing analysands. She then opened a joint psychoanalytic practice with her husband, Edward, in the late 1920s, and was elected a full WPV member in 1930/1931.

As a medical student, Grete Bibring spread an interest in psychoanalysis among her friends. One of them was Jenny Waelder-Hall. She may also have been influenced by Alexander Neuer, her sister Bettina's first husband, a Jewish psychiatrist and psychoanalyst from Vienna. According to their daughter, Ruth Neuer, Jenny Waelder-Hall admired Neuer (A. Bruckner and J. Bruckner, personal communication, January 6, 2021). Drawn to Freud by Grete Bibring, Jenny Waelder-Hall became a guest member of WPV in 1922 and an associate member six years later.

Marianne Kris had known Sigmund Freud personally since birth (M. Kris Nov. 15, 1972, pp. 1–2). He was a guest at her family home every weekend for a Saturday evening card party or a Sunday dinner with his wife, Martha Bernays. He is said to have picked Marianne's name shortly after her birth. Her intellectual interest in psychoanalysis started in her first years of medical school. She had wanted to undergo a personal analysis with Freud then, but he insisted on waiting until after her graduation. Then, they started a personal analysis with no fee that turned into a training analysis

(1931–1938, with several long interruptions). This concluded with Marianne Kris becoming a WPV member. She summarized her career choice in psychoanalysis as follows: "So it surely had its line from the identification with my father, and then I shifted it to the best friend, or one of the best friends, of my father" (M. Kris Nov. 15, 1972, p. 4).

Distinct among the women of the Black Cat group, Dora Hartmann did not become an analyst in Europe. Before emigration, she worked as a pediatrician in hospitals in Vienna and Heidelberg, publishing seven pediatric papers between 1927 and 1931, and opening a private pediatric practice in the 1930s. Her interest in psychoanalysis developed in the late 1920s through her husband and their friends: "Our closest friends at that time were the two Krises, [the psychoanalysts] Willi Hoffer and his wife, the two Bibrings, Helene and Felix Deutsch, the two Waelders – that was a very close group of friends" (D. Hartmann January 31, 1973, p. 9). Although Hartmann felt like "an outsider" who was "part of the group as Heinz [Hartmann's] wife, but not on [her] own" (26), she was in fact a part of it, contributing to the discussions at the Deutsches' home. She also attended IPA congresses when her parental responsibilities permitted, including in Wiesbaden in 1932 and in Marienbad in 1936 (her sons were born in 1934 and 1937), collaborating with Willi Hoffer, "a very close friend" (10), and referring children with psychological problems to his psychoanalytic clinic. Hartmann "started to have a lot of discussions [with Hoffer], analytic discussions, and he was the one who encouraged very much . . . to go into child analysis and to switch over" (10). She was arranging a training analysis with Anna Freud; however:

> [her] husband was very much against it at that time. He didn't want [her] to become an analyst, he felt that was a profession and he wanted to keep it way from his home. That was why [she] did not start analysis at all then (10).

Overall, the Black Cat women were not politically vocal; however, in prewar Europe the very choice to become a psychoanalyst was a political one. They were "naturally . . . deeply involved in politics" (Bibring April 17, 1976, p. 4). First- and second-generation analysts followed a calling, ignoring disadvantages that came with a profession that was neither prestigious nor lucrative: "It wasn't in fashion, it wasn't profitable, it was against odds for your future" (D. Hartmann January 31, 1973, p. 28). Analysts were ostracized in medical and academic circles. They were "outcasts." It was "absolutely impossible for a psychoanalyst" (24) to become a full professor. Prospective analysts were "an enthusiastic group of young rebels" (24) who wanted to be part of something new, groundbreaking and revolutionary. It was an "adventure" and an "experience, very exciting [that] made a difference, for everybody who chose to be there was really fully devoted to the hoping for learning something new – a new insight" (M. Kris Nov. 15, 1972, pp. 21–22). Psychoanalysis was a political project providing a new language to talk about issues that had not been addressed until then, striving to change stereotypes and supporting sexual emancipation of women. "We were a large group of liberal intellectuals and social democrats that is really involved in trying to help the working classes" (Bibring January 11, 1974, p. 9). Training analysts, aware that candidates in Vienna were rarely capable of paying fees amid the depression and inflation caused by the war, conducted work for no or for minor fees. "Oh I think I have never taken [payment] from an Austrian candidate" (Bibring May 11, 1973, p. 5). Each analyst was also obliged to treat at least one patient for free. Foreign patients were the source of income: "Dutch or English or American, they could pay, so this was really our source of income" (4). Bibring did not change her approach in the US, where she was purportedly called "one of the greatest bargains in Boston" (6).

Wives and Mothers

Female physicians who graduated from European medical schools before the Second World War often became romantically involved with colleagues of their age and married late for their time (see Freidenreich [2002] on this subject). The five women under study married prospective psychoanalysts of their age, except for Dora Karplus, who married Heinz Hartmann, eight years her senior (1894–1970). All married late for that period, with the exception of Grete Lehner (later Bibring). Helene Rosenbach married Felix Deutsch, her peer and a talented physician, when she was twenty-eight (in 1912). Jenny Pollak was also twenty-eight when she married Robert Waelder in 1930, a physicist, engineer and future lay analyst two years her junior (1900–1967). Marianne Rie married Ernst Kris, both at twenty-seven (in 1927), and he went on to become a distinguished art historian. Dora Karplus and Heinz Hartmann married in 1928 when she was twenty-six. Grete Lehner married Edward (Eddie) Bibring in December 1921 – she was only twenty-two and escaping her mother's strict rules, and he was five years her senior (1894–1959). The marriage was "a terrible scandal because one didn't do things like that" (Bibring January 11, 1974, p. 2).

Four of the women had become professionally interested in Freudian theory and entered psychoanalytic circles around the same time as their husbands. They then inspired and encouraged one another to enter personal and training analyses, and to become psychoanalysts. Heinz Hartmann was already an established analyst when he and Dora got married.

Their husbands, apart from Heinz Hartmann, were of Jewish descent. All had been born in Vienna, except for Edward Bibring, who came from Stanislau in Polish Galicia.

Ernst Kris, Robert Waelder, Felix Deutsch and Bibring lived significantly shorter lives than their wives. When Helene Deutsch died in 1982 at ninety-eight, Felix had died eighteen years earlier (in 1964). Jenny Waelder-Hall lived to ninety-one, until 1989; Robert died twenty-two years earlier, in 1967.[10] Marianne Kris died at eighty, in 1980; her husband and age peer died twenty-three years earlier, in 1957. Grete Bibring died in 1977 at seventy-eight; Edward died in 1959, of Parkinson's disease at sixty-five. The exception is Dora Hartmann who died only four years after her husband, she in 1974, Heinz in 1970.

The women bore children relatively late for their era. When Waelder-Hall first became a mother, she was thirty-four; Deutsch was thirty-three, Hartmann was thirty-two, and Kris and Bibring were thirty-one. Each, except Deutsch, had two children.[11] An important generational difference distinguishing the Jewish New Women from their mothers is that the latter had three children (the mothers of Hartmann, Kris and Waelder-Hall) or four (the mothers of Bibring and Deutsch). The children of Hartmann and Kris became doctors and psychoanalysts or psychoanalytic psychiatrists: Ernst Hartmann (1934–2013), Lawrence Hartmann (b. 1937), Anna Kris (1931–2019, later Anna Wolff) and Anton Kris (1934–2021). Both Dora Hartmann and Marianne Kris believed their children's choice of profession was influenced by their fathers, not by them. Both of Waelder-Hall's daughters became doctors: Dorothea (1932–1980, later Dorothy Hellman), an internist, and Marianne (b. 1933, later von Hippel), a pediatrician. There was a push from Waelder-Hall for her daughters to become physicians (von Hippel, personal communication, January 25, 2021). Martin Deutsch (1917–2002) graduated from MIT and became a leading nuclear physicist. Georg (later George) Bibring (b. 1929) is an engineer; his younger brother, Thomas (later Tom) (1932–2012), was a biophysicist.

Fleeing Hitler

Despite the succession of events in Germany that led to dictatorship and eventually to the Holocaust, which was mounting as Hitler was named chancellor in January 1933 and in short order included the imposition of emergency legislation after the Reichstag fire (February 1933), the first regular concentration camp, established in Dachau (March 1933), the first organized boycotts of Jewish businesses (April 1933), burnings of books (May 1933) and the imposition of the Nuremberg Race Laws (September 1935), Vienna-based intellectuals generally maintained an illusion that German fascism would be short-lived and felt relatively safe in Austria. The large majority of analysts in Austria in these years did not leave the country until after the Anschluss (March 12–13, 1938).

In 1933, Robert Waelder was one of few intellectuals in Austria who saw the handwriting on the wall. As "the only one who was politically informed" and who had a "very good political sense" (Waelder-Hall August 1973), he recognized the seriousness of the Nazi threat and urged his Black Cat friends to leave Vienna immediately for their safety in the face of Nazism and anti-semitism.[12] Ultimately, only the Deutsches were to follow his early advice, and even the Waelders remained to continue their work, hoping "that the impossible will happen" (Waelder-Hall August 1973). One factor behind Helene Deutsch's decision to emigrate was that she deeply worried about her son. She was "in the state of extreme anxiety about" Martin, who passed his *Abitur* in February 1935 at the age of seventeen, and was "filled with revolutionary zeal" (Deutsch, 1973a, p. 174) that might have meant trouble under the dictatorial regime established by Chancellor Dollfuss and in the aftermath of his assassination. Another factor was that Helene Deutsch had been actively searching for new professional opportunities beyond Vienna. When she first visited America in 1930, she immediately recognized it as "a haven for refugees persecuted in their own countries" (174). Their choice of Boston was determined by a job offer Felix had received from neurologist Stanley Cobb and the Massachusetts General Hospital. The job offer substantiated their visas. But Boston was a good fit for Helene Deutsch as well. There was a community waiting there for her, made up of émigré and American former patients, students and pupils. On her arrival, she also "had already filled up in advance almost all of [her] professional office hours with patients seeking analysis" (177).

In her memoir from 1973, *Confrontations with Myself*, Helene Deutsch wrote about her decision to emigrate: "nobody knew how terribly I grieved at having to leave not only Freud but also everything I held dear in psychoanalysis" (174). However, her private letters to her husband, Felix, who was forced to stay a few months longer in Vienna due to professional duties and joined them in January 1936, tell a different story. Within just a few weeks of reaching the US, she seemed to have left the past behind her and embraced her new home. She wrote, for example, about the "joyful liberation" from the "stupid, stuffy atmosphere" of Vienna (Helene to Felix Deutsch, Oct. 7, 1935), and the "dull, weary sickness" of Vienna "imprisoned in dreary brooding, turning around its own axis, . . . drying up and withering" (Helene to Felix Deutsch, 1935), "dull, narcissistic brooding" (Helene to Felix Deutsch, Oct. 18, 1935).[13] About those still in the sociopolitical cauldron of interwar Vienna, she wrote quite ruthlessly, "I feel sorry for my friends left behind – whom I personally love and esteem" (Helene to Felix Deutsch, 1935), suggesting that she has already detached herself emotionally from Vienna and the Psychoanalytic Society and Institute. Detachment, disassociation and denial were all strategies of dealing with guilt, shame, and loss and should not be judged. In the US, the highly successful career of Helene Deutsch continued. She helped organize the training of psychoanalytic candidates, worked as an analyst and served as president of the Boston Psychoanalytic Society (1939–1941). In 1944–1945, she wrote the monumental *The Psychology of Women* (Deutsch, 1973b).

The remaining four couples from Black Cat group all fled Vienna within weeks of Austria's annexation into the Third Reich in mid-March 1938. Jenny Waelder-Hall and Robert Waelder received a telegram from Helene Deutsch within days after the Anschluss, saying that she would sponsor them for a family visa. They left Vienna immediately after receiving their visas, traveling on May 31, 1938 to New York City aboard the SS *Île de France* (Husek, 1995, pp. 34, 56; M. von Hippel and K. von Hippel September 24, 2003; Ellis Island Passenger Records). Jenny Waelder-Hall decided to join her friend Helene Deutsch in Boston despite the strong pull to remain in New York from Lawrence Kubie, then co-chair of the Emergency Committee on Relief and Immigration of the American Psychoanalytic Association and later director of the New York Psychoanalytic Society (1939–1940).[14]

Already on the passenger liner's voyage to NYC, Jenny Waelder-Hall drew a hard line under the past. She said: "I was so disappointed in Nazi Vienna . . . that I completely detached myself from Vienna, there was no mourning Vienna, no sadness in connection with it, it was gone, dismissed!" (Waelder-Hall August 1973). According to the memory of her daughter, Marianne von Hippel, they "never saw [Jenny Waelder-Hall on the boat]. She just acted like in a depression or something, and I think that she was depressed because she thought that this is going to be the end of us" (M. von Hippel and K. von Hippel September 24, 2003). She also dissociated from the reality of being an émigré fleeing persecution, a refugee. She felt that she and her husband "did not come [to the States] as refugees but almost as tourists" (Waelder-Hall August 1973). She remembered that "people on the boat thought [her] a film actress because [she] was treated like a diva" (Waelder-Hall August 18, 1982). She was indeed greeted at the pier by a crowd of friends, including Helene Deutsch.

Jenny Waelder-Hall was determined to make Boston her new hometown as soon as possible. The fact that she came to the US with her husband and children, and that she reentered a community of friends, made it much easier. Having arrived in the company of her two American analysands returning from Vienna, one of whom was Helen Tartakoff (née Herlihy) (Tartakoff, 1975), another Elizabeth Kohut (née Meyer) (T. Kohut, personal communication, June 21, 2021), she did not have to reestablish herself professionally from scratch. By 1939, she was already very successful, "earning well, had a very nice house which she rented [in Brookline]" (Husek, 1995, p. 59). Jenny Waelder-Hall was one of the founders of the Baltimore-Washington Institute. She also helped set up the Association for Child Analysis in Michigan and the Psychoanalytic Training Institute in Miami. She published little, but was a very influential teacher in Boston, the Baltimore–Washington, D.C., area and Philadelphia.

It took the Krises and the Bibrings significantly longer to reach the United States. They first escaped Vienna to London, as part of the so-called Freud group – around a dozen people for whom Ernest Jones had arranged permits to live and work in the United Kingdom. They left Vienna by train on May 5 and 6, a month before Anna, Martha and Sigmund Freud left on June 4 (M. Kris Dec. 13, 1971, p. 11; Bibring and Hammer, personal communication, January 29, 2021). Grete Bibring is remembered to have kept everyone calm (Bibring and Hammer, personal communication,

January 29, 2021). Despite the escalating political tension and continued efforts by Jones, Marie Bonaparte and others to persuade Freud to leave, he had refused to flee even after the Anschluss. He finally gave in after the official dissolution of the Vienna Society by the Nazi authorities on March 20 (Nunberg and Federn, 1975, p. 303) and his daughter Anna was arrested by the Gestapo on March 22. He then requested that some of his editors leave with him, including Ernst Kris, the editor of the *Imago* journal since 1933, and Edward Bibring, an editor-in-chief of the International Psychoanalytic Association's journal *Internationale Zeitschrift für Psychoanalyse* since 1935.

In London, the friendship of the Krises and the Bibrings flourished. They rented houses three minutes' walk from each other, at 9 Marlborough Hill and 8 Carlton Hill, respectively, and less than a mile from the Freuds' house at 20 Maresfield Garden. All four of them joined the British Psychoanalytical Society and resumed seeing patients. For a little over a year, until Britain declared war on Germany on September 3, 1939, "the work was beautiful" (Bibring March 23, 1975). Shortly after, they sent all four of their children to a progressive boarding school an hour from London in the affluent village of Great Missenden (Kris Wolff January 21, 2018; Kris Wolff Nov. 13, 1986). The parents were stranded in London for professional reasons. Then, three weeks after the war started, Sigmund Freud died of cancer at the age of eighty-three on September 20, 1939.

Marianne and Ernst Kris departed with their young children for Quebec in July 1940, lived in Montreal for a few months and finally came to New York City in September 1940 on immigration visas arranged by the American psychoanalyst who had studied in Vienna, Ruth Mack Brunswick (M. Kris Dec. 13, 1972, p. 11). Marianne Kris recalls the trip as follows:

So we went [to Canada] with four destroyers around us and an airplane above for 24 hours to safeguard us. . . . [A]nd we arrived after a few days, but the ship on which we came was afterwards torpedoed, and sank, I heard. I forgot the name of it.

(M. Kris July 25, 1973, p. 49)

The interviews with Marianne Kris are filled with similar statements of "forgetting." It can be gleaned from them, as well as from conversations with her son, Anton "Tony" Kris, that she did not want to talk about the events of the war, Holocaust and emigration. When she did, she would often mix up dates, places and other details.

In the US, Marianne Kris was sought after as a child analyst, cofounded and served as first president of the Association for Child Psychoanalysis (ACP, from 1965) and was editor-in-chief of *The Psychoanalytic Study of the Child*, among other contributions. She gained fame as one of Marilyn Monroe's analysts.

Grete and Edward Bibring remained in London significantly longer than the Krises, not leaving until January 31, 1941 (Ellis Island Passenger Records). They were there during the intense mass air raids conducted by the Luftwaffe between September 1940 and May 1941. Late member of the Black Cat group Willie Hoffer became an air raid warden, and "every morning he went around, either by telephone or personally, to friends to see whether they are still there" (Bibring March 23, 1975). Several months before they finally left London, the Bibrings had received visas for the two of them through Mack Brunswick, but couldn't obtain visas for their sons (Bibring and Hammer, personal communication, January 29, 2021). Finally, after weeks and weeks of planning on how to help their friends, Jenny Waelder and her husband succeeded to arrange for an invitation for Edward Bibring from Albert Warren Stearns, dean of Tufts College Medical School in Boston, providing professional visas for the entire family. They were the last from the Black Cat group to arrive in the United States, doing so on the SS *George Washington*. An important factor facilitating emigration was that:

> when [she] came, [she] had a number of friends here, former students, colleagues. It was delightful to come to Boston and suddenly to discover how many of our friends were here . . . and they introduced us into their many ways of life.
>
> (Bibring, March 23, 1975)

In the US, she was a training analyst, president of the Boston Psychoanalytic Society (1955–1958), president of the American Psychoanalytic Association (1962–1963) and the first woman to receive a professorship in psychiatry at Harvard Medical School (1961).

Harvard Medical School waited almost hundred years to start officially admitting women after Elizabeth Blackwell became the first woman to enroll in a medical school in the US in 1847. In 1943, its all-male faculty first recommended the admission of women due to a shortage of male students because of the army draft. The first cohort of women students was admitted in 1945 on a ten-year trial basis. Eighty-eight women applied, and only twelve were accepted and matriculated.

Even though they had received US visas a day after the Anschluss, Dora and Heinz Hartmann initially emigrated to France. They left for Paris in April or May of 1938, soon after "a general discussion [among Freudians] where did one need analysts most, where should people go." According to Marie Bonaparte, "in France they were very badly in need of training analysts, and they were just begging Heinz [Hartmann] to come there and settle in Paris" (D. Hartmann January 31, 1973, p. 15). Many émigrés had already fled to Paris – a multicultural intellectual center that would seem welcoming and relatively safe until the Fall of France in June of 1940. Additionally, Nazism was probably not an immediate threat to the Hartmanns, since he was a gentile and she was Protestant who was married to a gentile.[15] While her husband was allowed to practice in Europe and immediately became very busy with English and French analysands from Vienna who had followed him to Paris and with new patients, Dora Hartmann, as a pediatrician, needed a French license to practice. Aware of the instability of the political situation, she decided to assume the role of homemaker (with the help of her Austrian housekeeper).

When the war began, the Hartmanns deemed it too dangerous to stay in Paris with two little children of two and five and left for Switzerland.[16] Switzerland was comparatively safe at that time; however,

> It was not too pleasant, you felt a little bit like in a mousetrap, you know. There was Italy under Mussolini – you were surrounded – in the south was Italy and on the east side was Austria, on the north side was Germany, that was all under Hitler, and on the west side was France, and to a great part the occupied part of France.
>
> (D. Hartmann January 31, 1973, p. 19)

In Geneva and Lausanne, Hartmann continued to take care of her children and the household. Once they decided it was time to flee Europe, they discovered that their visas had expired – they had not known that visas were only valid for four months after being placed in passports. By then, the Austrian immigration quota they were under was already full.[17] Friends helped arrange visas under the professional quota for qualified intellectual emigrants. The Hartmanns finally left for the United States in December 1940 by bus via southern France, Spain and Portugal, embarking by a ship from Lisbon and arriving in New York City in January of 1941. As with Waelder-Hall, Hartmann recalled "an extremely friendly welcome" (21). Their friends rented a hotel apartment for them, stocked up the "ice-box" with food and provided toys for the children. The Hartmanns chose to remain in New York, which resembled culturally diverse Vienna. Dora Hartmann graduated from the New York Psychoanalytic Institute in 1948. She was part of the ACP from its start, where she created a study group focused on drug problems in adolescence.

A Woman, a Jew and an Émigré in America

As psychoanalysts, Jews, women, Europeans, refugees and German-speaking emigrants, the women under study faced antisemitism, misogyny and racism.

Since they were driven from Europe by Nazi-led antisemitism and violence, Jewishness was an important component of the life stories of the women under consideration. However, antisemitic sentiments continued to afflict some of them in America. When looking for apartments to rent or buy, Jewish émigrés were often met with the racist practice of redlining. When the Deutsches bought a cottage in Cambridge, they were "greeted warmly with the words, 'We don't resent Jews like *you*!'" (Deutsch, 1973a, p. 188, original emphasis).

Grete Bibring encountered a gender-based pay gap. As the psychiatrist-in-chief of the psychiatry department at the Beth Israel Hospital at Harvard University, for a time she received the same salary as a fifth-year male resident.

They faced heartbreaking loss, a language gap, acculturation, and the need to reinvent and reestablish themselves in the new environment while handling mothering responsibilities. Grete Bibring summarized the difficult transition that marked her first years in Boston: "Oh God it was such difficult years" (Bibring April 11, 1976, p. 11).

There were also formal hurdles. In the United States, psychoanalysis was a branch of medicine. A medical degree and a medical license were required to practice psychoanalysis (with minor exceptions). European analysts with an MD had to pass a comprehensive, written state board medical examination in English to receive a state-issued license. As of 1938, twenty-one states required a foreigner to either become a US citizen, obtain an MD from an American institution or complete an internship before taking the exam. New York and Massachusetts were among the states allowing foreigners to take examinations without delay ("Bulletin of Information" 2012, pp. 32–37).

It took émigré doctors about two years to pass the exam and secure a license. However, even psychoanalysts with an American medical license were ostracized in medical circles of the era. Bibring felt that psychoanalysis was "enormously resented by the doctors" (Bibring April 11, 1976, p. 12). She suffered insults from other physicians.

However, overall, these five women promptly and successfully reestablished their careers in the US. According to the social rule of "migrant advantage," due to a combination of factors, emigrants of all races tend to be more resilient and resourceful than natives both in their home countries and in their adoptive countries (see Model, 2008, pp. 56–59 on this subject). The Black Cat women were mostly grateful to the United States for providing refuge and opportunities for professional growth. Grete Bibring stated: "I really like this country, I really always liked it, I never forgot how grateful I am for this country which is not affectation, not politeness, it is true" (Bibring April 17, 1976, p. 10).

Like almost all émigrés swept in this wave, they seemed very eager to assimilate, Americanize to a degree, and contribute to the American culture and society. They attended English-language courses and acquired cultural literacy. The process of adjustment was facilitated by the fact that there was a European, émigré, Jewish, psychoanalytic community waiting for them in the US. Helene Deutsch commented on her first weeks in the States: "Though I was still full of homesickness and a growing nostalgic desire somehow to go back, I was determined to speed up the assimilation process and began immediately to look for a home (Deutsch, 1973a, p. 178).

The relationship the Black Cat women had with Jewishness is complex. It is gleaned from her memoir and interviews that Helene Deutsch had chosen to identify as Polish and rejected her Jewishness. She recalled recurring debates on identity issues with her husband, a Zionist. It was a "never resolved . . . disagreement." Felix "regarded [her] nationality as Jewish; [she], as Polish" (Deutsch, 1973a, p. 197). It is clear from the interviews that Jenny Waelder-Hall may have rejected her Polish-Jewish identity in its entirety. For her, Polishness and Jewishness were linked, possibly due to the facts of the Second Polish Republic (1918–1939) being home to Europe's largest Jewish community by far, at some 3.5 million, and of the political antisemitism she had known in Poland. According to her grandson, Theodore von Hippel, she denied her knowledge of the Polish language and "she said that she wasn't Polish and had nothing to do with being Polish." Her daughter, Marianne von Hippel, added: "I didn't even realize until maybe in my adulthood that my mother had been Polish. . . . It was not something she was proud of. . . . She didn't [bring it up]. She was unhappy" (M. von Hippel and K. von Hippel September 24, 2003). Her sister, Helen, added that Jenny was "conscious about [being] Polish and *Jewish* Polish" to a point that made her "antisemitic." One time, she was supposed to have stated "I don't like the Jews . . . I mean the *Polish* Jews." On numerous occasions, when Helen would mention their Jewish roots, Jenny "was looking around that anybody hears that she's Jewish" (Husek, 1995, pp. 72–74, original emphases). Despite her resentment toward Vienna, Jenny Waelder-Hall introduced herself as born in Lemberg, Austria (versus Poland). Her close friend and psychoanalyst Jocelyn Malkin confirms: she "liked to think of herself as Viennese, she never thought of herself as Polish, always Viennese" (Malkin Dec. 14, 2000, p. 54). None of the women were religious as adults in any form.

Despite experiencing gender-based discrimination and antisemitism, for these women, gender and Jewishness were not key components in their professional life stories (see Chodorow, 1989 on gender salience). They identified first and foremost as doctors, psychoanalysts and professionals.

Still, the Black Cat women all held onto their European identities for a time by creating a "non-human environment" of objects that reminded them of home, along with Viennese customs and the German language (see L. Grinberg and R. Grinberg [1984] on this subject). How much was their sense of identity rooted in language? Helene Deutsch, Grete Bibring, Jenny Waelder-Hall and Marianne Kris all preserved their Viennese accents throughout their lives. Was it an unconscious attempt at preserving the European and Austria identity? Or was it a decision? Dora Hartmann's English was nearly perfect at the time of her arrival in the United States (L. Hartmann, personal communication, January 8, 2021). The Waelders, on the other hand, initially spoke German with their two daughters (von Hippel, personal communication, January 25, 2021).

Grete Bibring maintained the Austrian manner of addressing people, finding the first-name basis disrespectful and never accepting it. She missed the European habit of shaking hands to which Americans were then unaccustomed, and the elegance of wearing hats and gloves and carrying an umbrella (Bibring April 17, 1976, p. 14). According to their children, Kris, Hartmann and Waelder-Hall all dressed in a "European way": "unfashionable," "fairly conservative" and "old-fashioned" (A. Kris, personal communication, Dec. 27, 2020; von Hippel, personal communication, January 25, 2021). Bibring, meanwhile, always dressed in an elegant, sophisticated manner in tailor-made clothes. In Boston, she continued to host dinner parties, teas and Sunday brunches for friends including Anna Wolff and Anton Kris who, unlike their parents, lived in the Boston area (Jacobs and Umansky, 2015). The Hartmanns maintained some Viennese traditions, such as decorating the Christmas tree with food and actual candles. "They listened to music regularly . . . and went to concerts and the opera; and, especially in the early years in America, [Dora] occasionally sang, e.g. Schubert lieder, accompanied by [Heinz] at the piano" (L. Hartmann, personal communication, January 9, 2021).

Waelder-Hall had brought her children's mattresses to the United States, along with silver table service and napkins from Kaiser Franz Joseph's Vienna castle, bought when Austria-Hungary collapsed in 1918 and the castle's contents were being sold (A. Bruckner and J. Bruckner, personal communication, January 6, 2021). Kris brought her mother's paintings from Vienna. The Bibrings brought furniture and a piano that she kept in tune. The Hartmanns did not bring many possessions, just some books, furniture and clothing, but initially furnished their new home partly with European pieces from New York auction houses.

As is typical among many refugees, Grete Bibring refused to visit Austria, Germany or Italy after the war. Dora Hartmann also did not want to return to Austria, but was then persuaded by her sons to show them around Vienna in 1959. She, Jenny Waelder-Hall and Marianne Kris all returned to Vienna in July 1971 for the 27th IPA congress – the first one to be held in Vienna. Dora chaired one of the discussion groups and her son, Ernest, gave a presentation on sleep.

Epilogue

The Black Cat group did not come to the United States as a unit. After emigration to the US, the Black Cat group split between Boston (Helene Deutsch, Jenny Waelder-Hall and Grete Bibring) and New York (Marianne Kris and Dora Hartmann). The Boston bunch split again when the Waelders separated in 1940 and divorced in 1943, and Jenny Waelder-Hall moved to Washington that year (Robert moved to Philadelphia in 1940). Still, Helene Deutsch's "fantasy looked forward to the possibility of regrouping once more" despite "a long series of anxieties and uncertainties before [some of them] could revive their former attachments" (Deutsch, 1973a, p. 182). She and Grete Bibring had fallen out around 1941 when, while the efforts were being made to bring the Bibrings to Boston, Helene Deutsch worried about the ratio of analysts to patients and suggested that Grete became a housewife. The later took offense and their friendship never recuperated. Grete Bibring continued to hold her famous dinner parties, teas and Sunday brunches in Boston, like she did in Vienna and London. Her guests included Anna Wolff (née Kris) and Anton Kris who, unlike their parents, lived in the Boston area (Jacobs and Umansky, 2015).

Only New York-based analysts Marianne Kris and Dora Hartmann remained "intimate friend[s]" through sixty years, and met once a week (A. Kris, personal communication, Dec. 27, 2020) or "good friends for many decades, who saw each other regularly" (L. Hartmann, personal communication, January 8, 2021). Apart from Kris and Hartmann, in America the women under study went their separate ways.

Notes

1 I would like to express my deepest thanks to Olga Umansky, the librarian/archivist at the Boston Psychoanalytic Society and Institute, and to Nellie Thompson, the curator of the Archives and Special Collections of the Abraham A. Brill Library at the New York Psychoanalytic Society and Institute, for granting me access to archival materials, as well as to the children, grandchildren and the daughter-in-law of the analysts under study, each of whom were kind enough to talk to me and share family documents: George Bibring, Andrew and Judith Bruckner, Lawrence Hartmann, Anton Kris, Marianne von Hippel, Margot Hammer, Karin von Hippel, Theodore von Hippel, Kate Hartmann and Thomas Kohut.

   I will refer to the women under study using their married names, as this is how they chose to call themselves, not going by their birth names.
2 Much later, two more psychoanalyst couples, Hedwig and Willi Hoffer and Jeanne Lampl-de Groot and Hans Lampl, would join.
3 The category of an associate member was introduced in 1925. Associate members had supervision of full members.
4 For example, Margaret Mahler and Judith S. Kestenberg.
5 Jenny Waelder-Hall's birth certificate lists her father's place of residence as Stryhańce, a village in the rural commune of Roszniów (*Księga urodzin* 1898, 140).

6 With the exception of the medical faculty in Hungary under the Hapsburg rule started accepting women in 1896.

7 Lueger won four elections in two years, but Emperor Franz Joseph refused to appoint him mayor due to his antisemitic views. When Lueger won for the fifth time, his appointment was finally permitted.

8 The institute was established in 1924, though lectures and seminars did not officially start until January of 1925. Its forerunner was the International Committee on Psychoanalytic Training, also chaired by Helene Deutsch.

9 The remaining two were an endocrinologist and an internal medicine specialist.

10 Her second husband, Hessel Duncan Hall, an Australian historian of the British Empire, writer, naturalist and a gentile born in 1891 (seven years her junior), died thirteen years before her, in 1976. They got married in September 1943.

11 In Deutsch's case, choosing to have one child may have been dictated by miscarrying before giving birth to Martin.

12 Possibly also thanks to firsthand information from Waelder-Hall's sister, Bettina, who fled from Berlin to Vienna on February 27, 1933, the night the Reichstag was gutted in an arson attack.

13 All Helene Deutsch letters to Felix, as quoted by Roazen, 1985.

14 The Emergency Committee was established on March 13, 1938, and co-chaired by Kubie and Bettina Warburg in 1938–1939, and solely by Warburg until 1948. The committee worked to assist prospective émigrés with visas and jobs and new homes in the US (Thompson, 2012).

15 In Vienna, Hartmann had converted to Protestantism to avoid antisemitism (L. Hartmann, personal communication, Jan. 8, 2021). They were still targeted as Social Democrats and Heinz as a psychoanalyst.

16 The Hartmanns had Swiss passports. Heinz's grandfather had been a political refugee there from Germany. Heinz's father was born in Switzerland; both he and Heinz automatically received Swiss citizenship. Dora received a Swiss passport through marriage (D. Hartmann, January 31, 1973c, p. 16).

17 The 1921 Emergency Quota Act and the Immigration Act of 1924 set the total immigration quota at 164,667 for countries outside the Western Hemisphere (an 80 percent reduction from the pre-1914 average), and quotas for specific countries at 2 percent of the total number of individuals from each nationality that resided in the US (based on the 1890 national census). Generally speaking, the racist and antisemitic system favored white immigrants from Northern and Western Europe. It discriminated against those from Eastern and Southern Europe. In 1929, the quota was further reduced to 153,879, and specific national quotas were recalculated (based on the 1910 census). As a result, the German quota then fell by half (to 27,000). Poland, with its prewar Jewish population of 3.5 million, had a quota of 6,524. Moreover, the US State Department viewed quotas as limits, not goals, and did not fill them. The German slots were left unfilled until 1938.

References

1898. *Księga urodzin izraelickiego okręgu metrykalnego Lwów za rok 1898* [*Israeli birth certificate registry for Lviv region for 1898*].

2012. "Bulletin of Information to Be Supplied Only to Psychoanalysts Who Desire to Emigrate to the U.S.A." Appendix A to Nellie L. Thompson. The Transformation of Psychoanalysis in America: Émigré Analysts and the New York Psychoanalytic Society and Institute, 1935–1961. *Journal of the American Psychoanalytic Association* 60(1):32–37.

Bibring, Grete. (1974). "Dr. Grete Bibring Interview by Sandor Gifford." Oral History Transcripts and Oral History Interview Records, January 11, Boston Psychoanalytic Society and Institute Archives, Boston.

Bibring, Grete. (1976). "Dr. Grete Bibring Interview by Sandor Gifford." Oral History Transcripts and Oral History Interview Records, April 11, Boston Psychoanalytic Society and Institute Archives, Boston.

Bibring, Grete. (1976). "Dr. Grete Bibring Interview by Sandor Gifford." Oral History Transcripts and Oral History Interview Records, April 13, Boston Psychoanalytic Society and Institute Archives, Boston.

Bibring, Grete. (1976). "Dr. Grete Bibring Interview by Sandor Gifford." Oral History Transcripts and Oral History Interview Records, April 17, Boston Psychoanalytic Society and Institute Archives, Boston.

Bibring, Grete. (1973). "Dr. Grete Bibring Interview by Sandor Gifford." Oral History Transcripts and Oral History Interview Records, May 11, Boston Psychoanalytic Society and Institute Archives, Boston.

Bibring, Grete. (1975). "Interview with Dr. Grete Bibring by Dr. Oliver Cope, Psychoanalysis: A Personal View." March 23, From the Vault Grete L. Bibring Collection.

Bilewicz, Aleksandra. (1997). *Prywatne średnie, ogólnokształcące szkolnictwo żeńskie w Galicji w latach 1867–1914*. Wrocław: Wydawnictwo Uniwersytetu Wrocławskiego.

Bonnell, Marilyn. (1995). Sarah Grand and the Critical Establishment: Art. For [Wo]man's Sake. *Tulsa Studies in Women's Literature* 14(1):123–148.

Chodorow, Nancy. (1989). Seventies Questions for Thirties Women: Gender and Generation in a Study of Early Women Psychoanalysts. Chap. 10 In *Feminism and Psychoanalytic Theory* (pp. 199–218). New Haven and London: Yale University Press.

Czech, Herwig. (2018). Hans Asperger, National Socialism, and 'Race Hygiene' in Nazi-Era Vienna. *Molecular Autism* 9:1–43. https://molecularautism.biomed central.com/articles/10.1186/s13229-018-0208-6.

Deutsch, Helene. (1973a). *Confrontations with Myself. An Epilogue*. New York: W.W. Norton & Company.

Deutsch, Helene. ([1944–45] 1973b). *The Psychology of Women*. New York: Grune & Stratton.

Deutsch, Helene. (1973c). "Interview with Helene Deutsch." March 28, Oral History Interview Records at Boston Psychoanalytic Society & Institute Archives.

Deutsch, Helene. (n.d.). "Interview with Helene Deutsch by Lucille Ritvo." Oral History Transcripts and Oral History Interview Records, Boston Psychoanalytic Society and Institute Archives, Boston.

Ernst, Edzard. (1995). A Leading Medical School Seriously Damaged: Vienna 1938. *American College of Physicians* 122:789–792.

Freud, Sigmund. ([1900] 2010). *The Interpretations of Dreams* (James Strachey, Trans.). New York: Basic Books.

Friedenreich, Harriet Pass. (1996). Jewish Women Physicians in Central Europe in the Early Twentieth Century. *Contemporary Jewry* 17(1):79–105.

Freidenreich, Harriet Pass. (2002). *Female, Jewish, and Educated. The Lives of Central European University Women.* Bloomington and Indianapolis: Indiana University Press.

Gifford, Sanford. (n.d.). "P.S. by Dr. Gifford on Dr. Grete Bibring Interview." Oral History Transcripts and Oral History Interview Records, Boston Psychoanalytic Society and Institute Boston Psychoanalytic Society and Institute Archives, Boston.

Grand, Sarah. (1894). The New Aspect of the Woman Question. *The North American Review* 158(448):270–276.

Grinberg, León, and Grinberg, Rebeca. (1984). A Psychoanalytic Study of Migration: Its Normal and Pathological Aspects. *Journal of the American Psychoanalytic Association* 32:13–38.

Hartmann, Dora. (1973). "First Interview with Dr. Dora Hartmann by Dr. Stephen Firestein." January 31, New York, New York Psychoanalytic Society and Institute.

Holmes, Madelyn. (1984). Go to Switzerland, Young Women, if You Want to Study Medicine. *Women's Studies International Forum* 7(4):243–245.

Husek, Helen. (1995). "Interview with Helen Husek by Theodore von Hippel." June 8.

Husek, Helen. (1996). "Interview with Helen Husek by Judith Richardson Haimes." USC Shoah Foundation, June 1.

Interview with Dr. Marianne von Hippel and Her Daughter Karin [Mistakenly as Kristin] von Hippel, Sanford Gifford and Vivien Goldman, BPSI, September 24, 2003.

Jacobs, Daniel, and Umansky, Olga. (2015). *Grete Bibring: A Culinary Biography.* Boston: Boston Psychoanalytic Society and Institute.

Kris, Marianne. (1971). "Second Interview with Dr. Marianne Kris with Dr. Robert Grayson." December 13, Oral History Project of the New York Psychoanalytic Institute.

Kris, Marianne. (1972). "First Interview with Dr. Marianne Kris with Dr. Robert Grayson." November 15, Oral History Project of the New York Psychoanalytic Institute.

Kris, Marianne. (1973). "Third Interview with Dr. Marianne Kris with Dr. Robert Grayson." July 25, Oral History Project of the New York Psychoanalytic Institute.

Kris Wolff, Anna. (1986). "Interview of Anna Wolff." Oral History Transcripts and Oral History Interview Records, November 13, Boston Psychoanalytic Society and Institute Archives, Boston.

Kris Wolff, Anna. (2018). "Elizabeth Ann Danto interview with Anna Kris Wolff." Oral History Transcripts and Oral History Interview Records, January 21, Boston Psychoanalytic Society and Institute Archives, Boston.

Malkin, Jocelyn. (2000). "Jenny Waelder – Hall, M.D." Oral History Workshop #52, Part 5: Women in Psychoanalysis, December 14, American Psychoanalytic Association.

May, Ulrike. (2008). Nineteen Patients in Analysis with Freud (1910–1920). *American Imago* 65(1):41–105.

Model, Suzanne. (2008). *West Indian Immigrants: A Black Success Story?* New York: Russel Sage.

Nunberg, Herman, and Federn, Ernst (Eds.). (1975). *Minutes of the Vienna Psychoanalytic Society. Vol. IV: 1912–1918* (Margarethe Nunberg, Trans.). New York: International Universities Press.

Pauley, Bruce. (1992). *From Prejudice to Persecution. A History of Austrian Anti – Semitism*. Chapel Hill, NC: University of North California Press.

Rathkolb, Oliver, Peter Autengruber, Birgit Nemec, and Wenninger, Florian. (2013). "Forschungsprojektendbericht. Straßennamen Wiens seit 1860 als" Politische Erinnerungsorte. "Erstellt im Auftrag der Kulturabteilung der Stadt Wien (MA 7) auf Initiative von Stadtrat Dr. Andreas Mailath-Pokorny und Altrektor o. Univ.-Prof. Dr. Georg Winckler." 112–115. www.wien.gv.at/kultur/abteilung/pdf/strassennamenbericht.pdf.

Roazen, Paul. (1985). *Helene Deutsch. A Psychoanalyst's Life*. New York: Anchor Press/Doubleday.

Spector, Shmuel, and Wigoder, Geoffrey (Eds.). (2001). *The Encyclopedia of Jewish Life Before and During the Holocaust II and III*. New York: New York University Press, Yad Vashem.

Tartakoff, Helen. (1975). "Interview with Helen Tartakoff." Oral History Transcripts and Oral History Interview Records, Boston Psychoanalytic Society and Institute Archives, Boston.

Thompson, Nellie L. (2012). The Transformation of Psychoanalysis in America: Émigré Analysts and the New York Psychoanalytic Society and Institute, 1935–1961. *Journal of the American Psychoanalytic Association* 60(1):9–44.

Waelder-Hall, Jenny. (1973). "Jenny Waelder – Hall Interview." Oral History Transcripts and Oral History Interview Records, August, Boston Psychoanalytic Society and Institute Archives, Boston.

Waelder-Hall, Jenny. (1982). "Jenny Waelder – Hall Interview." Oral History Transcripts and Oral History Interview Records, August 18, Boston Psychoanalytic Society and Institute Archives, Boston.

Wolff, Larry. (2010). *The Idea of Galicia: History and Fantasy in Habsburg Political Culture*. Stanford: Stanford University Press.

Zeidman, Lawrence A. (2020). *Brain Science Under the Swastika: Ethical Violations, Resistance, and Victimization of Neuroscientists in Nazi Europe*. Oxford: Oxford University Press.

Websites

JewishGen: The Global Home for Jewish Genealogy. www.jewishgen.org/.
National Archives, Prague; Terezín Initiative Institut.
www.geni.com/.
The YIVO Encyclopedia of Jews in Eastern Europe. https://yivoencyclopedia.org.
www.psychoanalytikerinnen.de.

Part 2

Chapter 5

The Holocaust and Contemporary Psychoanalysis in America[1]

Emily A. Kuriloff

In many, many ways the calamity of the European Shoah simply fails, at least initially, to appear in the written record of psychoanalysis, both in Europe and its postwar revival in the USA. It is not as if it didn't happen, it is rather as though the topic is being reserved for another occasion, far from the analytic process and theory of the day. How then does a psychoanalyst – the researcher, historian, sociologist – work with scholarly material, historical documents and recorded testimony, and then elucidate the impact of the story on our ideas and praxis today? How to proceed? Even more to the point, how to proceed psychoanalytically? While the deconstruction of texts can prove useful at certain junctures, interpretation remains highly subjective and threatens to degenerate into a kind of armchair psychoanalysis that presumes too much, and, worse, pathologizes at every turn (p. 35).

We might begin suggesting that the predominantly Jewish analysts of the 1930s, vilified, marginalized and expelled from their homelands on threat of death, experienced difficulty holding a traumatic reality in mind alongside the life they had previously enjoyed and hoped to gain a new world. As Salman Akhtar (1999) notes, forced exile leaves little room for "nostalgic rumination, so that representations of the homeland itself are sent to psychic exile." Consider the Austrian-born analyst Heinz Kohut, who responded to a journalist's question regarding his theory of narcissism by referring to his own expulsion from Vienna in 1938: "I've led two totally different perhaps unbridgeable lives." It was this, he elaborated, that made him alert to "the problem of the fragmented self"(Quinn, 1980, in Kuriloff, p. 124). These statements imply that some degree of dissociation was one means by which many successful analysts managed memories of the unbearable anxiety and pain they suffered in Europe. Put differently, one reality would threaten the other.

DOI: 10.4324/9781003266228-8

We must not, however, assume that this or any other reaction to the trauma of the Holocaust was universal. Today's psychoanalytic sensibility, largely focusing on the individual in relation, challenges the assumption that catastrophic experience, or any experience, profoundly influences psychic life, provoking dissociation, enactment, or even more conscious avoidance and a narrowed psychic life. In her published memoir, for instance, Anna Ornstein's elaborate fantasy life helped her to tolerate the horror of Auschwitz, where she and her mother were imprisoned together. As she explains in her autobiographical book, *In My Mother's Eyes*, Ornstein passes a window and sees into "a little, warm space beyond the camp." She would imagine living there, a memory that "made the labor of walking in someone else's shoes, being hungry and totally exhausted, just a little easier to bear." Clearly, Ornstein's memoir does not support the assumption that trauma necessarily provokes dissociation and limits awareness. Nor does it suggest one's beliefs or sense of self are nearly as contextual or relativistic as many theories of dissociation have claimed. Instead, some essential identity, gleaned from our earliest and most intimate ties, sustains or exceeds the body and mind despite the pain of traumatic experience. As Kohut's student, peer and messenger, Ornstein spoke to her mentor's notion of a unitary self, less fragmented and less reliant on context than some other analysts theorize. In sum, to apply any single interpretation to a complex period of history discourages freedom of inquiry. Worse, it may result in a bogus psycho-history in which interpretative templates tend to be slapped onto the data willy-nilly. (Kuriloff, 2014, p. 3)

In the volume *Contemporary Psychoanalysis and The Legacy of the Third Reich*, I instead consider what Heidegger (1927) would call the "clearing" – a space that is metaphorical and shifting depending upon both the spatial and temporal. It is found as well as made, depending upon the nature of what is considered worthy of mention and the matter in which events are understood. During the time when many of the founding European analysts lived, private experience was considered less meaningful or useful to their work. Instead, the scientific, standardized approach to psychoanalysis was sought – an antidote to human misery. For many European analysts, objective standards also placed less emphasis on their marginalized status as Jews. Freud himself reckoned that if psychoanalysis became a valid and reliable method, so, too, might its practitioners. While today we honor the shifting subjectivity of an interactive matrix, in the early and mid-part of the 20th century, Jewish emigres analysts, attempting to render their theories and, by extension, themselves universally acceptable balked at any emphasis on context or the notion of a two-person psychoanalysis. Honoring the interactive matrix. Although they openly expressed the strongest kinds of loyalties and hatreds toward each other, such vociferous battles were waged under the guise of intellectual ferment, and any discourse linking ideas of praxis to a particular analyst's subjectivity was more or less taboo.

Most United States citizens, for instance, did not define themselves in the postwar period as having lived a trauma. They felt like the victors, not the victims. Typical of this was the treatment of the Anne Frank story. In her volume, chronicling the "afterlife" of a young girl's diary, author Francine Prose (2009) explains that the successful play and movie adaptation cut out the "dark side" – the Jewish stuff, the depressing stuff – emphasizing the feel-good part of the story. This was 1950s America. The war was over, the healing well under way. It was the time for the "sitcom team together with mom and dad and sis to head off to the secret attics" (p. 256). In the 1950s, Jews – even foreign-born Jews – felt more able to be complete and succeed in all areas in life than in any other time in the history of the United States. Why then would prominent physician/psychoanalytically trained émigrés focus on their upset and loss? Why should they not feel a new optimism? Indeed, the analyst Martin Bergman makes this very point in his edited volume dedicated to what he calls *the Hartmann era*, a period focused away from pathology and instead toward the development of a general psychology of mind and development. Bergman views this shift as representative of what he also calls a general optimism; an optimism born from circumstances in which "nearly all our participants in this moment were refugees from Hitler's Europe and had long waited for the Third Reich's defeat." When it came, Bergman asserts, it released hope and expectations. (Kuriloff, p. 77).

It was the Austrian Jewish emigre Heinz Kohut who created the first ripple within the hegemony of American metapsychology. The Viennese émigré, initially an apostle of Anna Freud, slowly threw off the shackles of a 1950s metapsychology in favor of the developing self. Thus, the shift from internal conflict to identity, a product of the quality of relatedness between parent and child, became paramount. Indeed, Kohut claims that his notion of narcissistic pathology, characterized by him as a divided self, emerged as a result of his war trauma, experienced as akin to a "before and after." As Kohut put it, "I have led two completely different lives" (Kuriloff, p. 40).

Heinz Hartmann

Heinz Hartmann, another refugee from Austria, was asked by an interviewer about the relationship between his personal experience and his ideas. He denied any such influence, except to emphasize his satisfaction with the success he found in America. Forced to relocate to Paris after the Anschluss, he and his family suffered Nazi bombing and hastily fled to America. Yet Hartmann responded to the interviewer's question, "Did you suffer from Hitler's oppression?" with "Not at all. No"(Kuriloff, p. 14). Indeed, the psychoanalyst Harold Blum has written that Hartmann's claim had been that he left Austria because he feared conscription into the German army. Part Jewish and married to a Jew, Blum instead says, "he probably would have been conscripted into a concentration camp." Blum says more about Hartmann's psychic strategy, described by him as a withdrawal from the external world. He takes as an example Hartmann's notion of the "conflict-free sphere of the ego" and the "average, expectable environment." When Hartmann wrote these things, Blum remarked, he was "surrounded by bay-onets, and about as distant from an average, expectable environment as one could be" (Blum, H. quoted in Kuriloff, p. 21).

Otto Kernberg

In an interview (Kuriloff, 2013) I conducted with the illustrious Jewish Austrian émigré analyst Otto Kernberg, he suggests that European ana-lysts who denied the fascist reality for as long as possible formed an iden-tification with the aggressor. This, Kernberg continued, later resulted in a totalitarian ambience in in post-World War II psychoanalysis, akin to what Kernberg refers to as German-Prussian control, a system to which the émigrés had previously fallen victim. Kernberg criticizes Hartmann, in particular, not only for his monolithic hold on post-World War II psy-choanalysis, but for his privileging only those theorists who were con-sidered Freud's direct descendants. "If a young analyst only quotes the senior people at his own institute, I don't mind," Kernberg explained to me, "but if everyone does it, including senior people, that shouldn't happen (Kuriloff, pgs.42–43). It's rigid; it has some elements of fascism. While the Holocaust, Kernberg asserted, was the organizing trauma of his life and his work, he also described "counting himself lucky" that his family fled to Chile, rather than to New York, so that he was free to think about ideas outside the narrow range of what was known as psychoanalysis in America. Kernberg explained that:

> As a young boy, we escaped from Austria to Chile. I was lucky to be trained at the small institute at the end of the world. I had a lot of good creative models before and during medical school and I read Freud and I dabbled too in Jung, who was interesting and complex. No one told me what was acceptable and unacceptable. However when it came to the U.S. I was really impressed by how regimented Freud's postwar psychology was.
>
> (Kuriloff, p. 41)

Over time, Kernberg's work brought together Freud's energic and structural models, developmental Ego Psychology, and the British Object Relations theories of Klein and Fairbairn. Indeed, Otto Kernberg and Stephen Mitchell were responsible for the revival of Klein in America. An America, once again, that fought tooth and nail to preserve what Anna Freud deemed psychoanalytic theory. As her bête noir, Anna rejected Melanie Klein's elaborations upon, and revisions to, her father's original ideas. Indeed, Kernberg broke through this orthodox, nearly sacerdotal stance, at first by revolutionizing the understanding and treatment of borderline patients and others with severe character disorders. Kernberg put it this way, "In the late 1960s and 70s, I began to notice the compatibilities between Ego Psychology and the British School." He was also impressed by Klein's elaboration, rather than her rejection many of Freud's principles. "I started writing and pointing to these links and I immediately came under attack." Kernberg goes as far as to suggest that his rejection of Ego Psychology as the only "true" psychoanalysis cost of his presidency of the American Psychoanalytic Association.

Martin Bergmann

Among the pioneers who dared to move away from American metapsychology, Martin Bergmann and Judith Kestenberg recognized the uselessness of focusing on intrapsychic conflict at the exclusion of the experiences of Holocaust victims. Unfortunately, however, Bergman did not consider such treatment to be psychoanalysis, but psychoanalytically informed supportive therapy. Put differently, the brilliant and innovative Bergmann held fast to metapsychology. When interviewing him, Bergmann was resistant to my notion that the scourge of the Holocaust profoundly changed the content and course of psychoanalysis. Instead, he commented, "My Jewishness, my immigration are meaningless topics. My oedipal rivalry with my famous father and with my analyst [Edith Jacobson] were the hate, pain, love, loss, competition and excitement" that preoccupied my psyche (Kuriloff, p. 24).

Yet, there seemed to be a shift in the nature of our conversation when Bergmann began to ask me less formal, more affect-laden questions. With undisguised pleasure, he exclaimed, "I don't know anyone in your generation who cares about this like you do!" I shared my family story, particularly my Polish-French family's odyssey, noting all that they had suffered and lost. We spoke of the difficulty of mourning. It was then that I dared to ask, "Ok so if my inner life is at work in my interest in the Shoah, what about yours?" Bergmann's expression immediately changed. "Oh," he replied, as if a light had turned on, "So you really know what's unconscious in this for me" (Kuriloff, p. 25). His office slowly became Heidegger's clearing, the space in which memories of love and loss could be had, and where he could speak of his European family. At one point, Bergmann showed me some of the "Yiddishkeit" in his office, including photos of shtetl Jews and other pieces of art. It bears mentioning that these photos and objects d'art dominated the room, evoking not only the Jewish European past, but it's brutal destruction as well. Bergmann's father, the famous Philosopher Hugo Bergmann, would tell Martin when he cried for seemingly no reason, "I am weeping for the kedoshim," Hebrew for the Holy Ones, those killed by the Nazis.

Dori Laub

The psychoanalyst and Holocaust scholar Dori Laub felt fortunate to have a Swedish analyst while a staff member at the Austen-Riggs Center in Stockbridge, Massachusetts – someone who was less defensive regarding the Jewish experience and response to the Holocaust. This analyst told Laub that he had known of liberated survivors who gave impossibly cheerful accounts of the concentration camps as they recovered in Sweden. They reportedly "claimed to have been made breakfast in bed at Terezin," for instance. He also described Polish women who said that the coffee at the camp was better than what they were given in Sweden after the war, where they were sent to recover. Laub himself remembers sharing a similarly sanitized view of the Shoah in his personal analysis. "My analyst," he explained:

> finally stopped my repetitive idyllic description of my childhood on the banks of the river Bug in Ukraine . . . because I was not able to know what really happened. In actuality we heard sounds of the Nazi death squad's guns killing screaming Jews on the other side of the river. Instead, I would play in a barren wheat field with another child, debating with her whether or not you could eat grass. Soon my analyst figured out this had something to do with hunger, because I was starving.

Yet Laub says that his analyst's interest in his experience was the exception. "Most clinicians didn't explore these things; it was all about infantile neurosis" (Kuriloff, 2014, pp. 15–16).

On the other hand, the work of Erich Fromm's interpersonal theory of conflict than that embraced by the Freudians. Rather than the chafing between desire and guilt, fantasy and reality, Fromm's notion of conflict concerns every individual's need to feel accepted versus the importance of being true to oneself. Indeed, this is how Fromm understood the ordinary German's willingness to go along with Nazi ideas, including some people he had believed were his close friends and colleagues. These people, Fromm later theorized, could not bear the possibility of social disapprobation and isolation from the mainstream should they side with the victims. Fromm's theory is thus a quintessentially interpersonal view of conflict. Indeed, Fromm's view of relatedness as that which determined what was possible for the individual is perhaps most obvious in 1940s Europe, an era in which hate and terror reigned. Other clinicians I interviewed who were trained in the interpersonal tradition, and thus similarly outside the classical mainstream, tend to speak rather directly of the ways in which the Holocaust and the Nazi scourge influenced their work.

Yet, paradoxically, we may find ourselves at the far side of the postmodern swing of the pendulum, in the midst of an overemphasis on the surround and at a loss for enduring concepts or theories of mind that transcend history. The testimony of Bergmann and Kris act as correctives to this inclination – reminders that thinkers and their theories may also transcend the moment and cast light and shadows to be considered alongside context. Again, a multiplicity of factors affected psychoanalysis during and after National Socialism, from both within and without its ranks.

If a straight line from the Nazi scourge to post-Holocaust psychoanalytic theory and technique cannot be drawn, consider that even those engaged in the "hard" sciences do not expect to follow crystalline paths toward singular results. Levenson (1972) quotes Bertrand Russell, who says, "I have wished to know how the stars shine, I have tried to apprehend the Pythagorean power by which numbers hold sway above the flux. A little of this, but not much I have achieved" (p. 217). Instead, exploring the governance of the universe, how people grow or, more specifically, the intersection between personal trauma and psychoanalytic discourse requires following what Levenson calls "the melody of change" (Kuriloff, p. 217).

Note

1 Parts of this essay are taken from chapter 1 of Kuriloff's 2014 volume, *Contemporary Psychoanalysis and the Legacy of the Third Reich. History, Memory, Tradition* (Routledge).

Bibliography

Akhtar, S. (1999). *Immigration and Identity: Turmoil, Treatment and Transformation*. New York: Aronson.

Bergmann, M. (1982). Recurrent Problems in the Treatment of Survivors and Their Children. In M. Bergmann and M. Jucovy (Eds.), *Generations of the Holocaust* (pp. 247–257). New York: Columbia University Press.

Bergmann, M., and Jucovy, M. (1982). Prelude. In M. Bergman and M. Jucovy (Eds.), *Generations of the Holocaust*. New York: Columbia University Press.

Fenton, J. (1995). A German Requiem. In H. Schiff (Ed.), *Holocaust Poetry* (pp. 104). New York: St. Martins Griffen.

Hartmann, H. (1964). *Essays on Ego Psychology: Selected Problems in Psychoanalytic Theory*. New York: International Universities Press.

Heidegger, M. (1962). *Being and Time*. (J. Macquarrie and E. Robinson, Trans.). New York: Harper Collins.

Kuriloff, E.A. (2014). *Contemporary Psychoanalysis and the Legacy of the Third Reich*. London and New York: Routledge (Quotes in this Essay are from this publication, unless otherwise noted).

Laub, D. (1992). An Event Without a Witness; Truth, Testimony, and Survival. In S. Feldman and D. Laub (Eds.), *In Testimony: Crisis of Witnessing in History and Psychoanalysis* (pp. 75–93). New York: Routledge.

Levenson, E.A. (1979). Language and Healing. *Journal of the American Academy of Psychoanalysis* 7(2):271–282.

Ornstein, A. (2004). *My Mother's Eyes*. Cincinnati, OH: Emmis Press.

Prose, F. (2009). *Anne Frank: The Book, the Life, the Afterlife*. New York: HarperCollins.

Chapter 6

Liberalism, Populism, and Mass Psychology

Eli Zaretsky

Introduction

Mass or group psychology is arguably the original or ur-version of political theory, as we see, for example, in Plato's *Republic*, where the tripartite character of the soul corresponds to the three social classes: workers, warriors, and philosopher-kings. One reason for the continuing power of classical political theory is that ancient Greece had no bureaucracy, no state in the proper sense of the term, so that the ruling class was essentially the citizens gathered together as a group. Nor was mass psychology restricted to Europe. Ibn Khaldun's *Muqaddimah* is a comprehensive explanation of the rise and fall of tribal or kin-based empires in terms of *asabiyah* or group spirit. In the modern world, mass psychology was reborn as the problem of the 'multitude," "mob," or "crowd" – forerunners of today's populism. The main modern theory of mass psychology – that of the Frankfurt School – was discussed and worked out almost entirely under conditions of exile and emigration, especially in the 1930s and 40s. At that time, the main expression of mass psychology seemed to be fascism, but psychoanalysis helped show that some of the group dynamics that underlay fascism existed in all societies, including the US.

The problem of understanding mass psychology has returned today, not in the form of fascism but in the form of the worldwide populist revolt, especially as represented by Donald Trump. In my view, the most striking political phenomenon of recent years has not been that revolt, but rather the inability of educated elites to understand it, including Trumpism. To move beyond that failure requires that we understand not just populism but also liberalism, and especially understand the relation between the two. This paper undertakes to do so by drawing on the tradition of mass psychology to explain not only populism but also liberalism. As I will argue, from

DOI: 10.4324/9781003266228-9

its beginnings, the liberal tradition divided between a mainstream wing that pathologized "the mob" and a progressive wing that engaged with the social movements of the era, especially socialism. I argue that the conflict between left and right, and the interaction between liberalism and the left, which the mainstream liberal/populism paradigm displaced, has to be restored.

How does mass psychology enter into this problem? In an established scenario, liberalism represents reason, which is an individual attribute, whereas populism represents unreason, lodged in the group. Populism, in this view, is liberalism's "other." But far from explaining populism, this view merely elaborates liberalism's own self-understanding. Something similar occurs in proto-sociological explanations of populism, such as those that revolve around globalization. In this view, globalization created a divide between mobile, educated, and cosmopolitan elites and provincial, often rural, left-behind working classes. The elites believe in diversity, while the left-behinds "cling" to guns and religion and embrace ethnonationalism. Whereas the cosmopolitans benefit from globalization, the ethno-nationalists, facing unemployment, get caught up in opioids. To be sure, there is truth in this account, but it smuggles in the standard liberal assumptions of elite rationality and mass unreason.

In truth, the concept of "populism" is itself a symptom of liberal confusion. Barely a concept at all in any strict sense, it is actually an amalgam of liberalism's intuitions and prejudices about its opponents: their irrationality, emotionalism, group thinking, demagogy, preference for the local and parochial, their resort to exclusionary ethno-nationalism on the one hand, and to the rhetoric of "class warfare," "a rigged economy," and "the people" on the other. At root, a displacement of the distinction between left and right, present-day understandings of populism are symptoms of liberalism's own disorientation. Far from offering explanations, they are attempts at self-justification. Far from clarifying the emergence of Trump and Trumpism, they muddy the waters.

In this essay, I want to suggest a different way of understanding the populist upheaval. My starting point is neither liberalism nor populism, but rather the theories of mass psychology generated by Sigmund Freud and revised by Wilhelm Reich, Theodor Adorno, Richard Hofstadter, and Christopher Lasch. In contrast to today's liberals, what is often termed Freudo-Marxism did not simply counter-pose liberalism to populism, or rather to the irrational mass psychology of their day, namely fascism. Instead, they discovered mass psychology, including the mass-psychological roots of fascism, within liberal, property-based societies themselves. Accordingly, they turned the tools of mass psychology inward – on "mass society" – including racism, xenophobia, and authoritarianism, but also on the supposedly democratic alternative to fascism, namely commodity culture. In short, they eschewed liberalism's self-validating assumptions and developed a mass psychology of liberalism itself.

Freud's theory of groups – the locus of the Freudo-Marxist tradition – developed in response to earlier theories of crowd or group psychology that were best represented by Gustave Le Bon, author of *The Crowd* (1895). Unlike Le Bon and other crowd psychologists, Freud did not contrast the putatively rational individual to the unthinking mob. Rather, he proposed his theory of groups in the course of developing a theory of the individual, namely the theory of the ego. In Freud's theory, the narcissistic cathexis of an "I" is the first step in the development of the ego. However, the ego is not the direct expression of narcissism; rather, it is a psychical structure or agency that contains a representation of the self within it. The ego's structure develops specifically through *identification* with "objects," beginning of course with the parents. Identification, for Freud, is not imitation but rather assimilation or incorporation on the basis of an unconscious wish. As the ego matures, it develops an ego ideal – a standard for judging itself and a "substitute for the lost narcissism" of childhood.

Understanding how the ego is formed is the clue to understanding groups. Groups form when "a number of individuals . . . put one and the same object in the place of their ego-ideal and consequently identify themselves with one another in their ego." Groups, then, are similar to dreams in that they are motivated by wishes, the difference being that with groups the wishes are collective. Thus, groups represent the utopian element in history. Freud also thought that the original or primal form of human life took the form of groups. He wrote:

the psychology of groups is the oldest human psychology; what we have isolated as individual psychology, by neglecting all traces of the group, has only come into prominence out of the old group psychology, by a gradual process which may still, perhaps, be described as incomplete.

Whereas Freud thought of his theory as trans-historical, his successors discerned a distinction between the mass psychology of authoritarian societies and that of democratic societies. The distinction can be inferred from the formula Freud gave for groups in general:

> the members of a group stand in need of the illusion that they are equally and justly loved by their leader; but the leader himself need love no one else, he [must] be of a masterful nature, absolutely narcissistic, self-confident and independent.

As this statement suggests, there are two directions along which the emotional life of a group flow. On the one hand, vertically or transferentially toward a leader or, we may add, toward a central symbol, such as an idea of nation, a deity, or a political principle like socialism or the like. Demagogues and dictators, such as Hitler, Mussolini, and Ataturk, and even conservative republicans like De Gaulle, fit this model when they drew on mass media, parades, sports events, and film to project themselves as father figures to enthralled nations. On the other hand, the emotional life of groups also flows horizontally, among the members of a group. Tocqueville's account of equality in *Democracy in America*, which stresses the ways in which citizens insist that no member of the group appear superior to any other, fits this model. "Democratic communities," Tocqueville wrote:

> have a natural taste for freedom; left to themselves, they will seek it, cherish it, and view any privation of it with regret. But for equality their passion is ardent, insatiable, incessant, invincible. . . . They will endure poverty, servitude, barbarism, but they will not endure aristocracy.

Liberalism was born in opposition to the new forms of mass politics that emerged with the English and French Revolutions. Liberalism was animated by what Ernesto Laclau called the "grande peur" of the nineteenth century: fear of the crowd. Contrary to Marx's hopes, the spread of capitalism did not usually produce revolutionary working classes. On the contrary, capitalism was accompanied by the mobilization of the masses, not just in the form of consumerism and mass culture, but especially around such non-rational, communal identities as nation, religion, and ethnicity. To understand such effects of capitalism, the Frankfurt School developed such concepts as reification, commodification, and one-dimensional or administered society. But such efforts ended in unresolvable antinomies. This was not the case with Freudo-Marxist mass psychology, which rested on a theory of instinctual motivation that was not easily manipulated or administered.

The need for mass psychology reflected the uneven development of capitalism. At one level, instrumental rationality and the market spread throughout the world, constituting the reality principle of capitalist society. At a deeper level, however, as Freud argued, in the shift from the predominance of the pleasure principle to that of the reality principle a species of thought-activity was "split off . . . kept free from reality-testing and remain[ed] subordinated to the pleasure principle alone."[1] This activity was phantasizing, which always accompanies the rational transformation of reality. Rather than developing in a unilinear fashion, the spread of capitalism was accompanied by a series of eruptions in the process by which the capitalist reality ego spread. The market system, and the liberalism that was so closely connected to it, needed to draw on these eruptions to gain a hegemonic place. Thus, liberalism drew on its own fantastic sources as well as projecting mass psychology onto the populist other.

The true theme that runs through the history of liberalism, then, is not the conflict between liberalism and populism, authoritarianism or "totalitarianism," as one often hears today, but rather an argument over the meaning of liberalism itself. At the deepest level, this is an argument between left and right. The important conflict in modern politics is not the conflict between liberalism and populism, but rather the conflict between liberalism and the left, working together, and the right, isolated from both. This conflict is often obscured in America's two-party system. The defeat or marginalization of the left – largely a product of the 1970s – and not the rise of populism lies behind the rise of Trump.

I will pursue this line of argument in three parts, which correspond to three moments in the history of liberalism: 1) classical liberalism, by which I mean essentially the British-led, Victorian liberalism of the nineteenth century; 2) social democracy, especially the New Deal; and 3) progressive-neo-liberalism – the liberalism of today's globalized, financialized consumer society. In each part I will center on the relation of liberalism to its mass psychological other. In the first part, I argue that what is today called populism is better understood as internal to liberalism – its "mass" or democratic element. In the second part, I argue that liberalism in the era of American hegemony (World War One to the present) successfully integrated the masses into a hegemonic liberalism through the building of the national state. The key to this success was the complicated and often fraught relationship of liberalism to a socialist and communist left. The development of a Freudo-Marxist theory of mass psychology was one product of the liberal/left alliance that characterized the World War Two era. In the third part, I argue that "progressive neo-liberalism" integrated feminism, gay liberation, and multiculturalism with market neo-liberalism in a powerful synthesis that rested on what Eizabeth Lunbeck has called the Americanization of narcissism. That synthesis excluded the left or, what comes to the same thing, redefined it in the form of identity politics and political correctness. Since 2016, the weakness of progressive neo-liberalism is well recognized in the loss of the white working class to Trumpism, evident in the Midwest and the South. The mass psychology of progressive neo-liberalism, not merely of working-class populism, explains this loss.

Part One: Classical Liberalism

It is best to begin with what Ernesto Laclau called liberalism's "*grande peur*," its fear of the masses. This fear reflects a tension inside liberalism. On the one hand, liberalism's critical innovation, which originated in Hobbes' *Leviathan* (1651) if not Machiavelli's *The Prince* (1513), was to break with ancient and Christian teachings in which government was the expression of "political man" (the ancient world) or "religious man" (the medieval). While Hobbes and Machiavelli themselves were no liberals, they were among the first to conceive of government as a "pure human device, rigorously external to everybody," in the words of Pierre Manent.[2] That made possible a new ideal of individual liberty, according to which individuals can pursue their own individual ends, which need not be political or religious at all. Liberal principles, such as equal respect for all individuals, follow from this ideal.

On the other hand, liberalism was also the expression of a rising social class: the property-owning bourgeoisie. In his 1962 book, *The Political Theory of Possessive Individualism*, C.B. Macpherson identified Lockean liberalism with the ideal of self-ownership.[3] In Macpherson's words, "Political society is a human contrivance for the protection of the individual's property in his person and goods, and (therefore) for the maintenance of orderly relations of exchange between individuals regarded as proprietors of themselves." Macpherson considered Locke in relation to the market, but a fully Marxist account must consider production relations as well. The liberal assumption, based on the market, was, in the words of DJ Manning, that:

> Excessive accumulations of wealth, power or opinion are direct threats to society's dynamism and equilibrium. Society generates within itself the energy that moves it in the form of human will, directed by reason. Compulsion is undesirable because the emotive force of progress lies in the spontaneity of the independent mind.[4]

But, as Moishe Postone argued, the Marxist rethinking of the economic problem in terms of socially necessary labor-time or value "is not simply descriptive, but delineates a socially general compelling norm." Production *must* conform to what Marx called "capital in motion."[5] *Pace* liberals, then, force or, to put it in psychological terms, *command*, was and is intrinsic to capitalism. Compulsive social forms, such as slavery, child labor, or colonialism, as well as excessive accumulations of wealth and power, are integral to capitalism, not contingent and avoidable wrongs.

At a superficial level, then, liberalism was based on exchange; at a deeper level, it reflected inequality, command, and friend-foe relations. Mass psychology, with its focus on irrational group formations and conflicts, studied the deeper level. This conflict within liberalism was apparent from the very start of the liberal tradition with the British response to the French Revolution. On the one hand, the Whigs, from which the British Liberal Party descended, opposed the older, aristocratic, landed interests in favor of individual liberties, "careers open to talent." On the other hand, they rejected "the revolutionary crowd" (*la canaille*), which propelled the revolution forward but also erupted into violence. Classical liberalism was defined by this ambivalence. Liberals celebrated enlightened, middle-class public opinion, underpinned by respect for property but castigated mass protests, the labor movement, and the revolutionary tradition.

Exponents of the liberal tradition based their understanding of mass psychology on what was often termed "public opinion" or "the tyranny of the majority," and, especially, "the crowd." As early as the French Revolution, middle-class thinkers invoked Mesmerism and "suggestion" to explain the new phenomenon of revolutionary crowd behavior.[6] Because liberals themselves supposedly acted rationally, *their* actions required no such explanations. Crowd or mass psychology applied only to their opponents, such as the Communards (Hippolyte Taine) or the criminal underclasses (Sighele, Le Bon). Carl Schorske's *Fin-de-siècle Vienna* demonstrated the tensions inherent in the liberal claim to rationality by describing how mid-century Hapsburg liberals erected a statue of Athena in front of parliament to reinforce the ideal of the rational citizen at the very moment the masses were entering the political process in the form of crowds, working-class strikes, mass demonstrations, mass or celebrity culture, and the new, "populist" – often antisemitic – politics.

The truth was that liberals feared the formless crowd but needed the crowd that it itself formed, through education, the army, the organization of labor, and especially through nationalism. With the growth of national school systems, armies, and newspapers, as well as great power politics in a new era of globalization, the distinction between the rational individual and the suggestible crowd became increasingly difficult to uphold. Every nation developed its own distinctive version of liberalism. In each case, it was fused with a new mass basis, such as national independence in Poland, anti-colonialism in India, or positivism in Mexico. German liberals supported the idea of a powerful nation-state. Even Russian liberalism became tied to the goal of national regeneration, especially after 1905. Different as these perspectives were, all of them sought to infuse what Gramsci called a national/popular element into liberalism, one that brought liberals uncomfortably close to what they were coming to call the masses.

The fusion of liberalism and mass politics culminated during World War One. The war, Zeev Sternhell has written:

> demonstrated the . . . facility with which all strata of society could be mobilized in the service of collectivity . . . [it] showed the importance of unity of command, of authority, of leadership, of moral mobilization, of the education of the masses, and of propaganda as an instrument of power.

With the war, in other words, the liberal "other-ing" of what was no longer the crowd but had become the citizenry largely ended, giving rise to a second phase in the history of liberalism: social democracy. The shift from British to American hegemony, a shift that coincided with World War One, coincided with the new fusion of liberalism with democracy.

Part Two: Social Democracy

Before World War One, the US was not liberal at all. Small Anglophile "liberal" currents supporting free trade and civil service reform did exist and the US had some characteristics, such as laissez-faire during the Jacksonian era, admired by British liberals. But it was not until the Progressive movement was born in the 1890s that the United States developed a counterpart to British liberalism. The true founder of American liberalism, Woodrow Wilson, was a devotee of the great British liberal Gladstone. Wilson opposed statism, which he identified with Theodore Roosevelt, but otherwise realized that American progressivism or liberalism needed a mass basis, which he identified with what he saw as the "natural" world of the market, which was not imposed, as he thought the state was. In Wilson's view, American Progressivism, or liberalism – the New Freedom, as he called it – was rooted in Jeffersonian democracy, which embraced the yeoman farmer and agrarian virtue while condemning central authority.

After World War One, the term "liberal" began to be used, partly to oppose Bolshevism and partly to signify "respect for the individual."[7] Building on Wilson's precedent, but also modifying it, Franklin Roosevelt redefined the term during the New Deal. Herbert Hoover called himself "a real liberal, not the anarchistic, communistic, socialistic type," but Roosevelt insisted the Democratic Party was the Party of "militant liberalism," adding collective security – economic and social as well as international – to the older meaning of freedom of contract. "Militant liberalism" incorporated a strong national-popular element, forging a cross-class coalition of immigrants, trade unionists, African-Americans, and the new organic intellectuals, such as teachers and social workers. Like a great army or host, the nation was called to follow a charismatic leader who utilized the new techniques of mass persuasion, especially radio, as well as monumental architecture, government-sponsored public works, campaigns of public mobilization (the "blue eagle"), a back-to-the-land ideology, romantic idealization of the people or "folk," as well as new material rewards through the expansion of the welfare states. Viewed in this way, the New Deal had much in common with the contemporaneous fascist states for whom "mass psychology," as it was then called, was the explicit method of rule.

The politicization of the masses in the New Deal era brought the psychological underpinnings of the liberal project to the fore. So long as liberalism was a restricted, middle-class phenomenon, the basis of freedom in the market was difficult to question. According to classic liberals like Adam Smith, and even Bentham in England and Madison in the US, the pursuit of one's economic interests was the essential component of rationality, understood in terms of means-end reasoning. This interpretation of liberalism also underwrote the broader idea that economic interests determine the nature and content of politics. While that idea went back to early British republican theorist like Harrington, Charles Beard's *The Economic Interpretation of the Constitution* (1913), which restated the earlier theory to portray the Constitution as the product of economic conflicts, especially those between creditors and debtors, was arguably the most influential single book defining New Deal liberalism in the thirties and forties.

As new forms of mass organization developed in both Europe and the United States, this rationalist, individualist psychology gave way to mass psychology. Thus, many liberals began to entertain the idea that their country was not only a class society, subject to economic exploitation, but also a mass society, subject to manipulation through "suggestion." The new mass media, especially radio and film, played an important role in encouraging this idea, as did new forms of collective organization, such as industrial unions. Film, Vachel Lindsey wrote, was "shallow in showing private passion [but] powerful in conveying the passions of masses of men."[8] More intangible but powerful too was the post-World War One longing for a "strong man," understood as someone who could control a crowd. In the 1920s, Mussolini's muscular frame and sexual prowess adorned magazine articles and, in 1928, Studebaker named a car the Dictator. During the thirties, however, as Americans became increasingly uneasy about their own tendencies toward regimentation and groupthink, the dictator became a repellent figure. In 1937, *Fortune* magazine explained:

> The [fascist] mass meeting is necessary if only for the reason that in it the individual, who is becoming an adherent of a new movement, [who] feels lonely, and is easily seized with the fear of being alone, receives for the first time the pictures of a greater community. [This shows] the magic influence of what we call mass suggestion.[9]

In 1939, John Dewey's *Freedom and Culture* warned that the real threat to America came not from foreign states but from "our own personal attitudes," which threaten to "give a victory to external authority, discipline, uniformity and dependence upon it."

Before the thirties, Americans had welcomed psychoanalysis for its association with sexual and cultural radicalism, but in the thirties, it became connected to mass psychology. This was especially the case with the Frankfurt School refugees who created Freudo-Marxian mass psychology.[10] They identified Freud's idea of the ego with the philosophical idea of the subject, as formulated in Kant's preface to *The Critique of Pure Reason* (1781). According to Kant, modern philosophy refuses to accept the world as something that has arisen independently of the knowing subject, and conceives of it instead as its own product. The Frankfurt School allied the free individual with the revolutionary tradition. According to Fred Weinstein and Gerald Platt's *The Wish to be Free* (1969), "the important development historically has been the strengthening of the ego." The development of the ego, therefore, and not the growth of the productive forces, or rationality as such, enabled bourgeois society's radical break with traditional authority in religion, politics, economics, and the family.

The New Deal era was a turning point in liberalism's relation to mass psychology. Instead of rooting the idea of a free individual in associationist psychology, instrumental rationality, and neo-classical economics, liberals began rooting their conception in group life in all its diversity, including working-class nativism, racial radicalism, immigrant ethnicity, and nation – "twentieth century Americanism," as the Communists called their program. As Warren Susman pointed out, "culture," the idea of a collective or organic way of life, became ubiquitous in the New Deal era. Overall, then, mass psychology became *internal* to social democratic liberalism. Liberals accepted that mass psychological processes like nationalism and democracy were necessary to incorporate and mobilize the masses. They adopted techniques of mass governance such as morale, propaganda, regimentation, and charismatic leadership.

In contrast to fascism and communism, however, the New Deal did not value the group per se. Rather, it valued democratic group processes that sustained a strong sense of individuality. This was the theme of many films of the Popular Front era, including *Spartacus* (1960), in which the individual confronts the tyrant-led mob; *The Ox-Bow Incident* (1943), a lynch-mob; and *Twelve Angry Men* (1957), an out-of-control jury. Many believed that the future of democracy depended on autonomous citizens socialized to oppose authoritarianism. As World War Two approached, an enormous literature on family, education, culture, and politics, all aiming to specify the psychological prerequisites of a democratic citizenry, also developed.

Part Three: Progressive Neo-liberalism

Progressive neo-liberalism, the third moment in the history of liberalism, began as a response to McCarthyism. Having watched entire peoples succumb to demagogic leadership and racial hate in Germany and Japan, Cold-War liberals termed the McCarthyist movement "populism" – a kind of internal exaggeration of the democratic process.[11] Richard Hofstadter, professor of history at Columbia University, introduced the term, redefining the nineteenth-century farmer's movement so that it conformed to his idea of the "paranoid disposition" – the disposition to see history as conspiracy and to center politics on "ultimate schemes of values" rather than on "negotiable interests." This was a key moment in eliminating the relevance of the Left and defining the opposition to liberalism as populism. Hofstadter's underlying assumption – still widely shared – was that paranoia was a weakness in the body politics and not something stirred up by anti-Communist liberal elites.

Cold War liberalism was an effort to contain and defeat the paranoid disposition, essentially by projecting ideological anti-communism outward. Like its predecessors – classical liberalism and social democracy – Cold War _liberalism rested on certain assumptions concerning mass psychology. These assumptions were self-congratulatory and projected irrationality outward. Economics, Cold War liberals explained, was rational because it was "trans-political." In contrast to Marxist "conspiracy thinking," which allegedly "saw capitalism everywhere," liberals encouraged pluralism, which held that "business" was merely one interest group among others. Cold War liberalism would also muffle those who would "use liberalism as an outlet for private grievances and frustrations," according to Arthur Schlesinger Jr.'s *The Vital Center* (1949). Most pregnant with meaning and complementing Hofstadter's deployment of the term "populism" was Schlesinger's urgent, parting advice: "that, in the interests of clear thinking, we abandon the word Left."

Cold War liberalism was never a viable politics and, in the event, was transformed into the more robust progressive neo-liberalism through its encounter with the democratic surge of the 1960s, especially the Civil Rights Movement, the New Left, and feminism. The movements of the sixties built upon the social democratic focus on collective action by stressing direct action, non-violence, and community organization. The result – participatory democracy – challenged the classic liberal paradigm of distributive justice, with its underlying assumptions of individual responsibility, by arguing that individual freedom could only be achieved through participation in groups. Witness the huge crowd formations for civil rights and peace in Vietnam; The War on Poverty, which called for "maximum feasible participation of the poor"; the be-ins; the demotic music and art; communes; the blurring of sexual boundaries; new art forms like happenings, Newsreel, and Living Theatre; "altered states of consciousness" (drugs); an activist culture, whose only regulative ideal was "participation;" and, perhaps of greatest importance in the long run, scorn for property. Herbert Marcuse's *Eros and Civilization* (1955) explained the new group experiences as a reversion to the primary narcissism of the mother/infant relationship. Such "oceanic" experiences took individuals out of their place in society and made possible the remarkable changes in personality and internal psychological constitution that we associate with the Civil Rights movement in the South, as well as with feminism and gay liberation.

It was especially the incorporation of feminism that consolidated progressive neo-liberalism. While the crowd formations of the New Left prepared the way for feminism, the new feminist "crowds" – demonstrations, consciousness raising groups, self-help, and women's health groups – differed from those of the New Left. Whereas New Left antinomianism generated "dis-identification" and a "shattering of social identity," the emotional drive in the seventies lay in *identification* – the basis for the building up of the self – and the mechanism of group formation. Women jettisoned older identities, which were redefined as patriarchal or heterosexist, and became "women-identified women," whether overtly as in lesbianism or in the sublimated form of women's loyalty to women. While the New Left had been universal but amorphous, feminists loosened the ties that bound women to men while strengthening the ties that bound women to one another, setting in motion a centripetal process of identity formation. The tighter the solidarity formed across the identity, the more it released self-assertion in its members. Cathy Cade, a documentary photographer, summed it up when she wrote that in the civil rights and anti-war movements, "I had been fighting for someone else's [freedom] and now there was a way that I could fight for my own freedom."[12]

The feminist revolution coincided with an epochal change in the character of capitalism. With the creation of a new global financial system in the 1970s, the US did what Great Britain did a century earlier. It relinquished its industrial primacy and encouraged its capitalists to invest abroad. In the words of Thomas McCormick, the US accepted its transformation into "a rentier nation, living off the income of its rents – that is to say, its direct and indirect overseas investments."[13] Manufacturing relocated to low-wage countries, leading to "deindustrialization," the "rustbelt," and "downsizing" – all terms invented in the 1970s. Labor unions were blamed for the great inflation of the period and, with the threat of capital migrating, began to accept weaker and weaker contracts. Michael Harrington's 1974 article, "A Collective Sadness," reflected on the lost sense of the meaning of work, while other authors evoked the new age of "limits," "diminished expectations," and "austerity." Rising poverty, declining real wages, and drug epidemics in rural America drove many workers despairingly to the right. Thomas Frank neatly captured the paradox of "small farmers proudly voting themselves off the land."[14]

Identity politics and neo-liberalism converged in the early seventies. The agent of convergence was new, privileged, educated elites who justified their privileges by the claim of being smarter, better educated, a more valuable form of "human capital," or by their control over credentials and licensing.[15] More important than property, they passed on to their children social and cultural capital, including access to the best schools (increasingly private), but also "taste," as in knowledge of food, wine, travel, fashion, and clothes. In earlier waves of capitalist expansion, the corrosive effects of the market had been recognized and "society," in Karl Polanyi's sense, sought to protect itself – for example through such New Deal programs as social insurance or protection for unions. Bucking the social democratic tide, a small group of self-described neo-liberals, centered on the Mount Pelerin society and including Walter Lippmann and Friedrich Hayek, sought to extend the market, not only into regulated or publicly owned areas of the economy, but even into previously sacrosanct areas, such as the family. Their utopian efforts remained marginal for decades, given the achievements of the New Deal and the understandable desire to protect society from the market. Only when the neo-liberals synthesized their outlook with feminism and gay liberation could such a far-fetched and counter-intuitive project succeed.

Feminism played a special role in this process because of its relation to the family, the lynchpin of morality and social cohesion. Feminists and neo-liberals converged in rejecting nepotism, the "old boy's network," and other gendered forms of privilege. Like feminism, gay liberation also rests on the weakening of the traditional family, as well as its reformulation in a neo-liberal guise. As sociologist Wolfgang Streeck wrote:

> the social and family structure that the standard employment relationship [i.e., the family wage] had once underwritten . . . dissolved in a process of truly revolutionary change. . . . The Fordist family was replaced by a flexible family in much the same way as Fordist employment was replaced by flexible employment, during the same period and also all across the Western world.

The progressive neo-liberal subject made explicit the psychological reason that linked liberalism to mass psychology. The neo-liberal subject could not be understood in egoistic terms – i.e., the pursuit of self-interest – alone. Egoism is a surface phenomenon. The embrace of egoism rested on the validation of narcissism. What Michel Foucault in *The Birth of Bio-Politics* (1977) called "productive power" – self-generated and self-managed, the essence of neo-liberal subjectivity – required a libidinal basis. Properly understood, the mind of the neo-liberal subject had three strata. Primary narcissism, or the "oceanic" feeling, a regression to the early relation to the mother prior to the institution of the reality principle was the most elementary stratum. The result of the transformative power of large group experiences, the availability of primary narcissism provided a new sense of fluidity and merger, visible in eco-feminism, feminist art, and attacks on the "Cartesian" ego.[16] Secondary narcissism expressed itself through group identifications, especially in the form of identity politics, which brought together persons with a distinct way of life and persons who belonged to a historically specific community. Egoism, self-interest, and calculation in the market, the third stratum, and the one closest to the surface, floated on a sea of narcissism. Any act, however, will combine motivations from all three strata.

The redefinition of the liberal subject in identity terms was accompanied by the revision – and ultimately rejection – of Freudian psychoanalysis. The revision began in the sixties when the New Left turned to Wilhelm Reich's reading of Freudianism as a revolutionary doctrine, which stood for the lifting of repressions and the freeing of instincts. In fact, Freud did not stand for the lifting of repressions per se, but rather for sublimation of the instincts, as can be grasped in his famous aphorism, "Where id was there shall be ego." In overturning the idea of Freudian or, as it was often called, Cartesian ego, the idea of an internal agency, intrinsic to the psyche as a whole and given over to self-reflective or critical thought, was lost. In its place, the ego was reduced to its market function; in other words, to egoism or "choice," or even "rational choice." As the ego lost its meaning, narcissism came into new prominence, but its political implications changed. Narcissism, in earlier liberal psychologies, had been associated with such non-marketable (because non-egoistic) domains as the family, art, nature, and romantic love. While sometimes derogated, for example by being associated with women, with homosexuals, or with passivity as opposed to activity, narcissism served as a utopian resource for critical thinking. With the progressive neo-liberal conception of the subject, however, narcissism and egoism were integrated into a single unit, collapsing the tension between them.

The Freudo-Marxist tradition survived, but now as a dissenting voice, especially in the form of Christopher Lasch's *Culture of Narcissism* (1978). Lasch's basic point was that the individual needs "the inhibiting, controlling and guiding function of the superego, which largely merges with the ego." Without a strong ego, internal values or principles lose their efficacy and the management of personal impressions or networking takes their place. In such a world, the individual with strong values and commitments is at a deficit, while the narcissist's ability to manage and manipulate impressions makes him or her a natural leader. At the same time, the primitive, irrational, punishing superego of early childhood lives on. To illustrate, Lasch drew on Joseph Heller's *Something Happened* (1974), the story of an advertising man plagued by impulses to kick or otherwise harm his fellow workers. With his children, he had always sought to be a "best friend," but they unconsciously regard him as a tyrant. He muses:

> I don't know why my son feels so often that I am going to hit him when I never do; I never have; I don't know why both he and my daughter believe I used to beat them a great deal when they were smaller, when I don't believe I ever struck either one of them at all.

We see the relevance of this in the aftermath of the student and feminist movements in the form of political correctness, and in American culture as a whole through the 1968 election of a law-and-order candidate – a forerunner of Trump – who claimed to represent the "silent majority" and mobilized large majorities against "rioters," "draft-dodgers," and "rich, white kids." A generation later, Richard Rorty warned that the working class may *"decide that the system has failed and start looking around for a strongman."*

To conclude, this brief overview is meant as an alternative to the many contemporary works that warn of the pathology of populism, authoritarianism, and right wing proto-fascism. It argues that from its beginnings the liberal tradition was divided between a conservative wing that pathologized "the crowd" and a progressive wing that engaged with the social movements of the era, especially socialism. In 1933, the Freudo-Marxist Wilhelm Reich invented the concept "mass psychology" to explain fascism, but his colleagues in exile, Adorno and Horkheimer, as well as Walter Benjamin, extended it to explain mass society in general. During the Cold War, American liberals adapted the term "mass psychology" to stigmatize all forms of supposedly irrational, "mass" or group-centered politics – communism to be sure, but also today's "populism." By contrast, I have argued that mass psychology, both as a phenomenon and as a theory, is intrinsic to liberalism itself, grounding it in social movements and mass politics but also rendering it unstable. From this point of view, the election of Donald Trump can be understood not as a challenge to liberalism, but as its complement or shadow.

Notes

1 Sigmund Freud, "Formulations on the Two Principles of Mental Functioning," in *The Standard Edition of the Complete Psychological Works of Sigmund Freud*. Translated from the German under the general editorship of James Strachey, in collaboration with Anna Freud, assisted by Alix Strachey and Alan Tyson (New York; Norton, 1976), XII: 222.
2 Pierre Manent.
3 MacPherson, 1962, pp. 263–264.
4 DJ Manning, Liberalism, 16ff.
5 Postone, article.
6 Crowds earlier.
7 Harold Stearns, Liberalism in America (1919).
8 Vachel Lindsey, The Art of the Motion Picture, 68.
9 Fortune, 1937, quoted Alpers, 108.
10 Reich.
11 The Populist Party of the 1880s–1890s in fact, its name notwithstanding, was not populist at all, but rather an example of Jeffersonian democracy. Contemporary scholars of populism, such as Michael Kazin, misled by the mere name, equate the Populist Party of the 1890s with populism in general, thus obscuring

the essentially populist dimensions of American liberalism. The name notwithstanding, the Populist Party of the 1890s was an expression of Jeffersonian democracy, not a forerunner of Juan Peron or even Donald Trump.

12 William Chafe.

13 Thomas J. McCormick, *America's Half Century: United States Foreign Policy in the Cold War and After* (Baltimore, MD: Johns Hopkins University Press, 1995), 164.

14 Thomas Frank, *What's the Matter with Kansas* (New York: Holt, 2004), 10.

15 Wallerstein, The Bourgeois(ie) as Concept and Reality. *New Left Review*, I-167, January–February 1988.

16 Two works widely read in the New Left era – Herbert Marcuse's *Eros and Civilization* (1955) and Norman O. Brown's *Life Against Death* (1955) – began to grasp this.

Chapter 7

Religion, Antisemitism, the Émigré Analysts, and Parallels to Our Time

Pamela Cooper-White

In this chapter, I will focus on antisemitism[1] and its role as I see it in the origins of psychoanalysis, and then reflect on some parallels to our present time.

I will begin by entering Freud's consulting room, that familiar historic image with its famous carpeted couch, every surface was laden with Greek, Egyptian and other ancient figurines, as is well-known. In fact, one scholar pointed out a little-observed fact that there were some ancient Jewish artifacts among his collection as well. With affectionate irony, he called them "my old and dirty gods" ("*meine alten und dreckigen Götter*") (Masson, 1985, p. 363). These figures represented to Freud, of course, his analogy between the process of psychoanalysis and an archeological dig.

That they were gods, however, presents a mystery never plumbed directly by Freud himself – suggesting the simultaneous fascination and aversion characteristic of a neurotic symptom. Both Freud's insistent atheism – he describes himself to his correspondent Oscar Pfister as a "completely godless Jew" (Meng and Freud, 1963, p. 63) – and his paradoxical obsessional return to the topic of religion throughout his cultural writings are well-documented. Less well-known, however, and even dismissed as unimportant, are the attitudes toward religion among the first analysts of Freud's Wednesday Night Psychological Society. Peter Gay (2006) tersely notes in his comprehensive critical biography that "Freud's view of religion as enemy was *wholly shared* by the first generation of psychoanalysts" (p. 533). As an academically trained academic, I find all such generalizations suspect, so it struck me as a vast over-generalization.

The first analysts had enthusiasm for complex and wide-ranging discussions about nearly every possible topic: history, philosophy, anthropology, religion across time and culture, and even the paranormal, as documented in

DOI: 10.4324/9781003266228-10

the minutes of this group and recorded by Otto Rank in their cultural journal *Imago* and in other published works, correspondence and memoirs. I spent a semester as a Fulbright scholar at the Freud Museum in Vienna working with these primary sources. My first hypothesis was that the group's views might be more complex and less strictly conforming to Freud's later views on religion than was previously assumed. What I found, in fact, was a rich and often more nuanced view toward religion among Freud's early follow-ers than has generally been recognized. I have detailed many examples in the book that originally came out of this research, *Old and Dirty Gods: Religion, Antisemitism and the Origins of Psychoanalysis* (Cooper-White, 2018). I'll summarize here the main ways in which they had their own com-plex ideas and didn't just follow Freud's ideas to the letter.

They did, of course, often apply oedipal interpretations to ancient civili-zations' ritual practices, as Freud himself did in *Totem and Taboo* (Freud, 1955/1913). And they critiqued the repressive, moralistic teaching of the Viennese Catholic Church, which was absolutely hegemonic and closely entwined to the Hapsburg monarchy. They saw the teachings of the church as masochistic. But, at times, they also expressed quite original ideas about the positive role of religion in advancing the sublimations and compromise formations necessary for civilization – a variant on Freud's *Civilization and Its Discontents* (Freud, 1961a/1930), and quite different from *The Future of an Illusion* (Freud, 1961b/1927), by which time Freud posited religion as "virtually the enemy of civilization" (p. 6). They believed that religious faith could be protective against neurosis and even suicidality. The Swiss analyst-pastor Oscar Pfister further argued that psychoanalysis was com-patible with a liberal and non-repressive version of a positive Christianity, freed from the constraints of moralizing dogma. These first findings would have been more than enough to say, "Mission accomplished!" based on my initial hypothesis.

But a second, unanticipated thesis emerged as a result of this study, which I believe in the long run is more important. That thesis is that the surround-ing atmosphere of antisemitism, well before the rise in power of the Nazi movement, stands at the *fons et origo* of psychoanalysis. Antisemitism shaped the first analysts' ethical sense and was formative in their theory as a desire to analyze *from the underside* what lay beneath every surface of the human psyche. Obviously, there is no one impetus behind the develop-ment of psychoanalysis, yet with its curling tentacles, antisemitism was one of the most pervasive forces in twentieth-century Vienna and it could not have failed to inform the thinking of Freud's circle, both consciously and unconsciously.

Antisemitism can be thought of as an ocean of ancient hatred in which the first analysts, almost all of whom were Jewish, had to swim throughout their entire lives. It took constant vigilance to survive, much less succeed, in its dangerous waters. Antisemitism therefore stands as a *"total context"* (a term from sociolinguistics and anthropology) – an ineradicable overarching reality that could not have failed to influence these first analysts' discoveries and explorations, and without which their theoretical insights could not be fully understood. The first analysts' experience of being a perennial "Other" of Austrian and German culture could not have failed to infuse their theorizing with a desire to analyze from the underside of both the human psyche and of society. It should come as no surprise then that their theorizing about repression would focus on the twin drives of sex and aggression. These not only emerged as the underlying causes behind clinical cases of neurosis, but sex and aggression were hallmarks of the dominant Viennese culture. Sex and aggression were the continual "return of the repressed" in Vienna, which subversive Expressionist artists depicted more frankly.

There was a miasma of decay emanating from the grand, pseudo-historic façades of the *Ringstrasse* (the central, circular street encompassing the central district of Vienna and representing the emperor's grand ambitions). Sex and aggression appeared everywhere and nowhere in *fin-de-siècle* Vienna. Young girls dressed in virginal white made their society debuts at the vertiginous January balls, while Schnitzler's *süsse Mädel* ("sweet girls") survived while entertaining the same girls' fathers in backstreet apartments. Government positions and aristocratic titles were bestowed in backroom deals. Sex, power, exploitation, and violence were denied and hidden, like the nude bodies Gustav Klimt painted and then covered over with ornate geometrical designs. The repressed in Vienna was an open secret. And beneath the mannered airs that made everyone appear to be an aristocrat, Jews became the repository for gentile Austrians' projections of their own envy, greed, sexual hungers, and inferiorities, as Sander Gilman (1991, 1993) and Jay Geller (2007) have shown us. Vienna was burning from the inside with the fever of its own hysterical contradictions.

Freud's Jewishness has already been well-examined as a dynamic factor in the development of psychoanalysis, yet Jewishness itself of course is not identical with antisemitism. The very long shadow of antisemitism itself must also be located as a catalyst at the very origins of psychoanalytic theory and practice, in terms of what the first psychoanalysts could see that no one else was seeing. The core realization of psychoanalytic thought – that there is always more beneath the surface of psychic reality, and that this *more* is, among other things, affective, memory laden and psychological – cannot have failed to have had something to do with the experiences of the first Jewish analysts in their position of marginality, occasional elusive successes and chronic persecution.

Antisemitism is a belief system saturating the dominant culture of western Europe, delineating the Jew as "Other." The Nazis conducted pseudoscientific studies comparing ethnic physiognomies in order to prove the superiority of the Aryan race as compared to Jews and other groups – e.g., Africans and Roma ("gypsies"). As Dutch psychoanalyst Hans Reijzer (2011) has observed, "When people live in between two cultures, they think dialectically and see society dynamically" (p. 25). The Jews of Austria could understand the language and culture of both oppressed and oppressor, and they also could not fail to view and judge themselves through the lens of the dominant culture. The famous Swiss psychiatrist C.G. Jung experienced culture shock on his first visit to Freud's Wednesday Night Psychological Society, and viewed the Viennese analysts, in his own words, as "cynical" (Bair, 2003, p. 118). But in their own context, that was simply what came of being awake to the societal dynamics into which they were born. It was part and parcel of surviving in a hostile environment.

Yearning for acceptance and assimilation was one psychic force, which sometimes engendered both denial and hope. Realism and the knowledge of ever-present danger was the countervailing force. The former, the assimilationist story that psychoanalysis is generally just a Western science is the narrative we hear most often. The latter – the subversive knowledge of oppression – is the uncanny truth of trauma that returns again and again in disguised form but can never remain entirely repressed. Long before Nazis were lined up, weapons in hand, blocking the entrance to the University of Vienna, long before there were explicitly antisemitic clubs all over university life, this oppression was always brewing.

So, to turn to parallels to today, having been immersed in the history of Austria and Germany between the world wars, I have watched the nightly news ever since the election of Donald Trump to the U.S. presidency in 2016 in what feels like a kind of time warp. "Now" is beginning to feel a lot like "then." As a psychologist of religion, I see how religious hate and extremism is exploited in our own time as it was in the run-up to World War II, with roots going back centuries. At the end of World War I, the Germans and their allies were punished severely by the terms of the Treaty of Versailles. They had lost over three million soldiers during the war, and at the end of the war, people were impoverished by a decimated economy, literally starving and further ravaged by the Spanish flu that swept the continent and killed Freud's daughter Sophie. Sophie's son Heinz, Freud's beloved grandson, died three years later of tuberculosis. A profound global economic depression followed, and ordinary people who were neither politicians nor military leaders, but who were simply ground up by the consequences of war, found it easy to view themselves as victims. Hitler's rhetoric of nationalism and making Germany great again, irresistibly filled a vacuum.

People blamed the more liberal democratic government – the Weimar Republic in Germany – along with Jews, socialists and communists, for collaborating with the Allied powers and betraying the German cause. This was called the "stab in the back myth" ("*Dolchstoßlegende*"). Whipped up by Hitler's charismatic racial rhetoric, people's previously more private antisemitic words and deeds found permission to be released as overt hate speech and violence. Hitler's bizarre blend of pseudo-Christianity and folklore, with Wagnerian opera as its grand art form, invoked a shared cultural narcissism on a massive scale. Gradually a consensus grew, and it seemed less and less shocking – all the while rationalized by scientists, the lawyers, anthropologists and Hitler's brand of psychologists – to "purify" the Aryan nation by gathering together, then deporting and finally killing all Jews along with the also long-hated Roma, homosexuals, person with disabilities, Marxists, and resistance fighters. For the Jewish upper-class professionals and intellectuals, it seemed impossible to comprehend.–

Like the proverbial frog in the pot of boiling water, as the heat was turned up, all too few – including Freud himself – realized the extremity of the inferno beneath their cultured feet. Some, like Freud, often with the help of influential outsiders, escaped with their lives. Six million Jews – two-thirds of the European Jewish population, including four of Freud's own sisters – were murdered.

So consider the parallels today. Americans have sent and continue to send millions of young family members into combat overseas. Poor and working-class families, especially since the end of the draft, have sent their loved ones and received a disproportionate number of flag draped coffins and wounded warriors back. Countless families cope with the invisible wounds of PTSD and moral injury. We recently lived through a Great Recession and job loss, and the economic fears of the working class are exploited by right wing demagogues. Our common public discourse glorifies war and warriors, while at home oppressed groups, including both persons of color and women, still fight for basic equality. It's easy for middle-class Americans to view themselves as victims, and Donald Trump's rhetoric of nationalism, "Making America Great Again" and the "Great Lie" of a stolen election in 2020 is irresistibly filling a vacuum. Trump's followers continually blame the liberal Democratic government, Wall Street (which again invokes the antisemitism against Jewish financiers), and immigrants for taking away their jobs and destroying the comfortable middle-class white America, with the apple pie, picket fences and Yankee Doodle patriotism that they thought they could rely on – as well as a distorted white-supremacist, right-wing Christianity that bears virtually no resemblance to authentic Christian theology but has been manufactured in cynical alliances between power-hungry evangelical leaders and power-hungry conservative politicians (Cooper-White, 2022). Whipped up by Trump's charismatic, racist, Islamophobic and, yes, antisemitic propaganda, people's previously more private racist words and deeds found permission to be released as hate speech and overt violence. And, in the past three years, the entire world has again been plunged into a pandemic that, much like the Spanish flu of 1918–1919, has cost hundreds of thousands of lives in the U.S., Europe and across the globe. The resulting malaise has only added to the fragility of democracies in the U.S., Europe and elsewhere. We are once again living in dangerous, burning times.

Rabbi Irving Greenberg (2000) once wrote, "The Holocaust confronts us with unanswerable questions, but let us agree to one principle. No statement, theological or otherwise, should be made that would not be credible in the presence of the burning children" (p. 27). Taking into consideration years of mounting fear, the eventual terror of forced migration and an aftermath of often intense survivor guilt, from its beginnings psychoanalysis was riddled with an often repressed but uncanny return of an innumerable crowd of unlaid ghosts. How might psychoanalysis, which seeks truths beneath the surface – however turbulent, however irrational – help us to find a way forward past the pandemics of racism, xenophobia, antisemitism, the metastasis of right-wing lies across social media and the multiple threats to democracy posed by authoritarian strongmen here and abroad? If we are not living in 1933 or 1938 in the America of today, we are certainly living in a time when democracy is as imperiled as it was during the 1920s in Europe, with its first stirrings from authoritarianism to outright genocidal dictatorship. What can we learn from the forced migration of psychoanalysis itself from Europe to the U.S. during the Holocaust?

Beginning with Freud's Viennese Circle and continuing on from the first generation of analysts in Europe across the globe, psychoanalysis still bears this multigenerational wound. Antisemitism and the Holocaust are its deepest scar and stain – a persistent, still un-metabolized trauma at the heart of the discipline. One consequence of all this un-metabolized trauma may be that, of all the psychotherapeutic disciplines, psychoanalysis has been among the slowest to recognize the impact of context on the psyche, both at the level of individual patients' sufferings and at the level of society. It wasn't always that way. Although Freud's shift in emphasis from the impact of real traumas in the environment toward inner conflict and repressed desires tended to downplay external traumatic realities, the total context of antisemitism and the first analysts' efforts to resist its penetrating logic of denigration also informed and shaped their ethical sensibilities and a vision of resistance and social justice. Many early analysts engaged in movements for social and political reform between the wars. For example, Anna Freud and her generation's work with the Red Vienna movement resulted in free clinics, kindergartens, housing projects and healthcare for the poor of the city (e.g., Danto, 2007). This perspective was left behind during the flight to America, even suppressed for the sake of assimilation and survival, by most émigré analysts who fled Nazi persecution during the 1930s and 40s (Jacoby, 1983). The émigré analysts soon found themselves facing yet another authoritarian threat in the form of McCarthyism, as Ellen Wolf Schrecker (2021) has detailed in Chapter 2 of this volume.

This trend toward assimilation was of course motivated by survival and post-traumatic fear. And it occasioned the natural idealization and even fossilization of the world that was lost – so common among all immigrants and refugees, including a rigidifying of so-called "Classical theory," as Emily Kuriloff (2014) has so carefully researched as summarized in the Chapter 5 in present volume.

Assimilationism reinforced secularism and, moreover, as Melanie Suchet (2007, 2016) has pointed out, resulted in a whitening of Jewish analysts, who in Vienna were still regarded as racially other: Jews were called "*Schwarzen*" (Blacks). There was relief in leaving behind sheer terror, but the positive spirit of resistance and perspicacity from the margins that the early analysts embodied was also left behind, and Freud himself acknowledged a useful analytical distance from the so-called "compact majority." As Russell Jacoby (1983) wrote of the transplantation of psychoanalysis from Europe to America, "The psychoanalytic texts endured, but the spirit and culture vaporized. Americans who did not experience the European chapter accepted a reduced psychoanalysis, devoid of its politics and culture, the whole enterprise" (p. 7).

Just as in the last decade, relational analysts have begun to bring the attention of psychoanalysis as a field to issues of race, class, gender, sexuality, and politics, and even as spirituality and religion have finally begun to be admitted into some psychoanalytic discourse (e.g., Aron, 2004), a turn or, more accurately, *re*-turn toward context begs the question of how context already did really matter to the first historic generation of analysts. This should recall the historic, immersive reality of antisemitism into our present awareness. Holocaust survivor Eli Wiesel, who died in the summer of 2016, was known for his passionate exhortation that we must never forget the horrors of the Holocaust, lest we repeat them. We appear to be immersed in a period of history in both the United States and Europe that feels eerily similar to the emergence of hate speech, violence and right-wing – even fascist – demagoguery that preceded the Holocaust in Europe. How can psychoanalysis, with its deep appreciation for the impact of history, especially repressed history, help facilitate Wiesel's project of staying awake in the face of rising terror?

Note

1 I use the spelling "antisemitism," following Ostow (1996), to avoid the pseudo-racial 19th c. terms "Semite" and "anti-Semite/ism."

References

Aron, L. (2004). God's Influence on My Psychoanalytic Vision and Values. *Psychoanalytic Psychology* 21(3):442–451.

Bair, D. (2003). *Jung: A Biography*. Boston: Little, Brown.

Cooper-White, P. (2018). *Old and Dirty Gods: Religion, Antisemitism, and the Origins of Psychoanalysis*. London and New York: Routledge.

Cooper-White, P. (2022). *The Psychology of Christian Nationalism: Why People Are Drawn in, and How to Talk across the Divide*. Minneapolis: Fortress Press, 2022.

Danto, E.A. (2007). *Freud's Free Clinics: Psychoanalysis and Social Justice, 1918–1938*. New York: Columbia University Press.

Freud, S. (1955). Totem and Taboo. In J. Strachey (Ed.), *Standard Edition of the Complete Works of Sigmund Freud* (Vol. 13, pp. 1–162). London: Hogarth. (Orig. publ. 1913).

Freud, S. (1961a). Civilisation and Its Discontents. In J. Strachey (Ed.), *Standard Edition of the Complete Works of Sigmund Freud* (Vol. 21, pp. 59–146). London: Hogarth. (Orig. publ. 1930).

Freud, S. (1961b). The Future of an Illusion. In J. Strachey (Ed.), *Standard Edition of the Complete Works of Sigmund Freud* (Vol. 21, pp. 5–56). London: Hogarth. (Orig. publ. 1927).

Gay, P. (2006). *Freud: A Life for Our Time*. New York: W.W. Norton.

Geller, J. (2007). *On Freud's Jewish Body: Mitigating Circumcisions*. New York: Fordham University Press.

Gilman, S. (1991). *The Jew's Body*. New York: Routledge.

Gilman, S. (1993). *Freud, Race, and Gender*. Princeton, NJ: Princeton University Press.

Greenberg, I. (2000). The Shoah and the Legacy of Antisemitism: Judaism, Christianity, and Partnership After the Twentieth Century. In R. Frymer-Kensky, D. Novak, P. Ochs, D. Fox Samuel, and M.A. Singer (Eds.), *Christianity in Jewish Terms* (pp. 25–48). Boulder, CO: Westview/Perseus.

Jacoby, R. (1983). *The Repression of Psychoanalysis: Otto Fenichel and the Political Freudians*. New York: Basic Books.

Kuriloff, E.A. (2014). *Psychoanalysis and the Third Reich: History, Memory, Tradition*. New York: Routledge.

Masson, J.M. (1985). *The Complete Letters of Sigmund Freud to Wilhelm Fliess, 1887–1904*. Cambridge, MA: Belknap/Harvard University Press.

Meng, H., and Freud, E.L. (Eds.). (1963). *Psychoanalysis and Faith: The Letters of Sigmund Freud and Oskar Pfister* (E. Mosbacher, Trans.). New York: Basic Books.

Ostow, Mortimer. (1996). *Myth and Madness: The Psychodynamics of Antisemitism*. New Brunswick, NJ: Transaction Publishers.

Reijzer, H. (2011). *A Dangerous Legacy: Judaism and the Psychoanalytic Movement* (J. Ringold, Trans.). London: Karnac.

Schrecker, E.W. (2019). Presentation to the Conference: "The Emigré Analysts and American Psychoanalysis: History and Contemporary Relevance," Sandor Ferenczi Center/New School, New York, December 13.

Suchet, M. (2007). Unraveling whiteness. *Psychoanalytic Dialogues* 17(6):867–886.

Suchet, M. (2016). Facing Our Racialized Selves. NYU Postdoctoral Program in Psychoanalysis and Psychotherapy Diversity Conference, New York, January.

Part 3

Chapter 8

The Exile Within

Irene Cairo

Introduction

This essay has a self-reparatory aim.

It is the product of my 50 years as an immigrant; years when I rarely reflected on the impact of that experience. Thus, when invited by Adrienne Harris to contribute to The Émigré Analyst Conference at the Ferenczi Center in December 2019, I realized immediately that the subject that became my contribution then, and evolved into this chapter, seemed to have been present in my preconscious, awaiting the opportunity to be articulated for a receptive audience. That subject is an amalgam of reflections about memory and memories, forgetting and remembering, nostalgia, identification, and identity.

My specific focus is the meaning and processing of memories for that special category of migrant: the exile.

I find Nancy Hollander's (1998) definition of exile most accurate and poignant. She says: "Exile is a specific form of migration, without yearning, and shorn of hope and aspiration."

My conjecture is that, for the exile, when there is no possibility of return, there is both a conscious effort and a powerful unconscious need to suppress, ignore, or "delete" memories.

Such a process is not only unlikely to be successful but reveals itself to be quite fragile, thus exposing the exile to an unexpected, sudden, and often violent and painful eruption of those memories. Memories that have been purged, so to speak, for the same reason that drives political purges: the danger of an upheaval.

Not surprisingly, even when the process is moderately successful, the subject pays a price in the loss of other aspects of their mental life together with those that were targeted for repression.

DOI: 10.4324/9781003266228-12

My reflections were framed, as must be obvious, in the context of my own experiences.

Personal Background

In their erudite, charming, extensive exploration of multilingualism, "The Babel of the Unconscious" (1993), Amati Mehler, Argentieri, and Canestri affirm that, inevitably, when talking about multilingualism, all authors talk about themselves. I believe the same is true of the subject of immigration and exile. I am no exception.

Not only am I an immigrant but my four grandparents were immigrants into my native Argentina. Thus, I grew up with multiple stories of various and contrasting places, cultures, countries, and continents, as well as with inevitable curiosity about the experience of moving countries.

I learned about nostalgia from my maternal grandparents. Since they both had left before the Russian revolution of 1917, they believed they would never go back. Perhaps that made them romanticize some memories. It would take many years of successive revisions for me to appreciate the complexity of their experience.

My own experience in moving to this country is very different from that of any of my grandparents, since I did not come to the United States with the intention, or even the fantasy, of staying in the country.

I will highlight an event that crystallized my conflicted relationship with my immigrant status.

In 1978, when already eligible to become a citizen for many years, I travelled to Argentina for a week. There I had an unpleasant – in no way dangerous, just unpleasant – bureaucratic experience. In great contrast, when returning to New York, the US immigration officer at JFK examined my documents, and then affably stated: "everything is in order, welcome home."

That simple expression shocked me and moved me with its profound symbolism, forcing me into the sudden awareness that this indeed *was now home*. There was no other. This country was quietly claiming me. The event precipitated my decision to apply for naturalization.

I would be hard pressed to define what I believed myself to be *before* that incident, but certainly I could not describe my inner status as that of an immigrant.

Thus, I only gradually became aware of a condition in which I remained for many years: my national identity had been submerged in ambiguity.

I most certainly was not American, yet I was no longer Argentinian. I lived in a sort of "national identity limbo" and, much more dramatically, there was minimal space in my mind to reflect about the topic.

Such ambiguity makes for a very special vulnerability.

As I will try to show later, even for the immigrant whose motivation was not exile, there is often an identification with the exiles from the same country. Such identification may subvert the achieving of an adaptation to the new country. Such identification allows the immigrant to maintain an internal preconscious connection with the old country that is partly false, being based on a sort of "borrowed" identity.

Those words "borrowed identity" evoke the notion of deceit, of illegality. Yet that immigrant with the borrowed identity is innocent of any crime. There is no other victim but herself.

This takes me to a consideration of very specific social aspects of this issue.

Exile, of course, is the consequence of social and political events. Perhaps then it is also necessary to frame my thoughts in the context of my history and my views about political involvement and social action.

It is in this particular context that my subject has a very personal relevance and history.

As a medical student in Buenos Aires, Argentina, I spent many hours at the home of a classmate and friend whose parents were Austrian, the father a surgeon, the mother a psychoanalyst. My memories of their hospitality and warmth also involve fragments of their stories. I knew they had left Austria "just in time" before the Holocaust, and that they had fought in the Spanish Civil War. My friend's mother had been in training at the Vienna Institute in 1933. She had been known to be a Communist Party member. When the government made the Communist party illegal, her analyst, Richard Sterba, informed her that "the Professor" – as Freud was referred to – had suggested that if candidates wanted to continue their training, they should forsake all political activity. (Later it was revealed that this was not Freud's idea, but Federn's.) As she would tell years later, Marie (Mimi) Langer thought that whereas "psychoanalysis may be the most important thing in my life" it would not survive the triumph of fascism. At that point, Sterba decided to report that her analysis was sufficiently advanced for her to graduate, thus allowing her to avoid the dilemma she faced.

The story is told in her moving biographical work, "From Vienna to Managua, Journey of a Psychoanalyst." This extraordinary woman would still face similar situations many years later. One of the founders (with Angel Garma and Arnaldo Rascovsky, among others) of the Argentine Psychoanalytic Association, she would leave that institution, and also the IPA, in 1971, with a statement of radical principles that declared psychoanalysis and Marxism were not only not incompatible, but both essential for the development of man. Not long after that, endangered by her ideas vis a vis the Argentinean state terror, she would migrate to Mexico, where she continued working, and from where, many times, she traveled to Sandinista Nicaragua to teach psychoanalysis. Psychoanalysis, and her political world view, formed the core of her identity.

That is the world into which I "grew up" as a physician, as a therapist, as a psychoanalyst.

That is the background against which I made the decision to work for human rights organizations formed to protect people in my native country, where tragic events were then taking place.

Some 40 years after Marie Langer faced the choice of a psychoanalytical career or political activity, a married couple of training analysts at the institution she founded in Buenos Aires (the APA) had their 16-year-old son, who had attended a high school meeting, kidnapped by the paramilitary organizations that were the main tool of state terrorism. The news, murmured at first, soon shook up the institution. Soon their analyzands, mostly candidates, all knew about this event. To maintain any connection with a member of a family that had been marked as a target for the organizations of state terrorism meant a risk that could result in kidnapping, torture, and death. Both analyst parents analyzed the possible masochistic reasons for their analyzands to continue their analysis with their endangered analysts.

This was the culture I came from. This was the world I was geographically far from but emotionally close to.

While such horrors were taking place, I was privileged to live in this country, where Argentine state terror could not reach me personally. I was privileged to maintain an involvement in Argentine politics from a distance. Such involvement protected me to some extent from my status as an immigrant. In some part of my mind, I remained in Argentina. But the worst aspect of that false status is that I did not know it. Such a partial identification with those who remained in Argentina was both a shelter and a trap; a trap that hid my version of "survivor's guilt." Like others in a similar situation, I lived in relative alienation from dissociated parts of myself.

Theoretical Background and Discussion

In 1989, Leon and Rebeca Grinberg's book *Psychoanalytic Perspectives on Migration and Exile* appeared in Spanish, and was translated into English in 1992.

In reviewing it for *Psychoanalytic Books*, I commented that I found it astonishing that the subject of migration had never been looked at from a psychoanalytic perspective, particularly because the experience of migration has been so closely intertwined with the dissemination of psychoanalysis. It seems evident now that the conflicted relationship to the subject by the protagonists of those migrations could not yet be approached.

In contrast, today immigration has become a subject for many distinguished psychoanalytic authors. A very profound thinker among those is Salman Akhtar, who has been addressing many aspects of the process since 1995, particularly the pathology of immigration. He has focused on the role of nostalgia, identity formation, identity diffusion, and transcultural conflict. I will later refer to specific aspects of his contribution.

In 2004, Judith Skeracs-Weiss and Ivan Ward edited an extraordinary book, *Lost Childhood and the Language of Exile*. In it, writing about the paucity of pertinent literature, Leon Kleinberg states "perhaps it is too painful and personal to write about." This is a true, but I would say timid, statement, as immigration is clearly an experience that is *always* personal and almost invariably painful.

Revealing the personal impact and the edge of pain in the experience, Skeracs-Weiss writes: "soon I started seeing patients in London. The difficulties began literally at the door. The Hungarians shake hands, in London people do not."

It is easy to find many other colleagues for whom similar experiences were deeply disturbing.

And whereas I emphasized that for the exile the conditions of memory and memories, remembering and forgetting are clearly, as Akhtar affirms, different from those faced by the immigrant, I want to frame what follows in a particular reflection.

We think about exile as being the product of political events, now a dramatic contemporary fact. Nearly 70 million people were displaced in the world at the end of 2018. Yet the impossibility of return is not only linked to politics. Two of my four grandparents, "economic" migrants from the great Italian current of immigration to Argentina at the beginning of the

20th century, would not imagine, after three months on a ship, that it was possible to return to their native land.

A major difference, however, always resides in the fact that for the exile, terrible events have *preceded and accompanied* the experience of leaving the native country. Life under terror has already left scars and demanded an emotional price.

Thus, in part, the success of adaptation will depend on the emotional balance achieved in the present between the painful memory of the past experiences in the original country and the new, hopefully positive experiences building in the new country.

In this regard, it is useful to remember Nancy Hollander's (1998) thoughts, where she states "exile is the human experience in adulthood that most clearly recapitulates the infant's experience of attachment, separation and loss."

My ideas about memory for the exile are different from Akhtar's (1999) ideas on nostalgia and closer to those of Andrew Harlem (2010). Akhtar believes that nostalgia and idealization are "remedies" used by the immigrant against the difficulties of adaptation to the new country. He affirms that nostalgia helps the immigrant to defend against the aggression resulting from current frustrations.

Whereas I see the logic of his thinking, and agree that *sometimes* that can be observed, there are two important distinctions that I want to make in regard to both idealization and aggression. The first: idealization is, invariably, a *fragile* defense, and thus it does not help for long. What is being avoided through idealization is the *mourning* process that is necessary and key for eventual adaptation. Whatever the reasons for leaving the country of origin, certainly what makes for a radical difference in the experience is indeed the impossibility of return. I add that such impossibility is not only derived from political circumstance, but it may be due to natural disaster or economic issues. Many immigrants other than exiles will never have the opportunity to return.

It is that impossibility that requires a process of mourning that is essential.

My second distinction regards the role of aggression. I believe that healthy aggression is quite useful and, on occasions, is essential for psychological survival. The aggression often mobilized by the violence that precipitated the exile may be channeled into social action that results in being strengthening and adaptive.

I now turn to Harlem. He writes:

> the (im)possibility of return in determining the psychological course
> of the migratory process is unquestioned. . . . Delineating between the
> immigrant and the exile based on these factors seems vital . . . but I have
> conceived of this distinction on another basis . . . the exile is not simply
> one who cannot physically return, she is someone who cannot "remem-
> ber" other versions of herself, who cannot bridge the gaps between
> versions of self that are rooted in disparate time, physical spaces, and
> relationships . . . someone who "cannot stand in the spaces" between
> self-states.

This is, in my view, a key distinction that subtly delineates the internal
processes that were disrupted. I venture that those processes are also latent
for many other immigrants, as the experiences of adaptation to the new
country, the growth and changes of the personality in the context of the
person's foreignness, do not follow a maturational chart, but occur in what
sometimes seems seismic movements.

Clinical Illustrations and Discussion

So, now I come to the illustration of my ideas about the way that those dis-
ruptions in the processing of memories occur, the way in which the broken
pieces of identification are suddenly shaken, and pieces are reconstructed,
or constructed anew.

I will give two examples. Both from my analytic practice.

The first from a foreign young woman. Celeste, a pediatric nurse in her
late twenties and an only child, came into analysis following the death of
her mother in her native country. She had briefly returned to her country
when receiving news of her mother's illness. She had stayed for a period of
time but had to return to her job in New York. When the mother died shortly
after she had left, she scheduled a trip for later in the year, so as to plan and
take a longer vacation and visit with her father.

Her analysis progressed through what seemed like a natural process of
mourning, with the complexities of such a process, into an exploration
in greater depth of her intense, profoundly affecting relationship with her
father. Unattached at the beginning of the analysis, she soon began to date
men, and at the same time developed an interest in a hobby that had been

very important to her father – an identification that was protective in the mourning that would follow.

About a year later, Celeste's father died.

She had begun a relationship with the man she would eventually marry, a man from her native county. Unlike her, his situation was such that he could not return, and thus Celeste resolved that she would not return at that time either.

Celeste married and finished analysis with the idea that there may be issues that she still may need to work on.

Two years later she returned with intense anxiety. The political situation in the country had changed and she had now returned with her husband.

On the return flight to New York, looking out of the window on the plane, she had seen clouds that looked eerily like the faces of her parents. She knew this was an illusion, but she was immensely affected and could not stop sobbing on the plane, with the irrational thought that this was "a message." A few weeks of sessions revealed that the impossibility of return for two years, including her not being at the father's funeral, had led to a "freezing" of many memories, associations, and ideas, many centered around that hobby of the father's that she had undertaken – memories, associations, and ideas which had flooded her on the plane back to New York. The identification with the situation of an exile, because of the husband's political situation, had also protected her from a different kind of mourning process.

I will now go on to my other example, which involves a very personal experience.

In 1985, the report on the disappearance, torture, and murder of victims of state terrorism in Argentina, "Nunca Mas" (Never Again), was published.

For all of us, it evoked intense emotional and sometimes physical reactions. For some of us, it meant that we had to carefully guard against the irruption of terrible images and the invasion of suppressed associations. When we washed our faces on a cold winter morning, we may have thought of water boarding; when we accidentally ripped an edge of a fingernail, we may have seen nails being pulled; when a spark flew from the gas stove, we may have smelled skin being burnt; when we made love, we may have had pictures of cattle prodders introduced in vaginas or anuses. And so on.

But then, we had to go into our offices, hopefully "without memory or desire," and we probably blocked more than would have been ideal with the aim to stay open to our patient's projections.

Thus, we come to the particular session I will describe.

Betto was 26 years old when he started his analysis, which lasted seven years. Lonely, incapable of a love relationship, suffering severe obsessional symptoms, and exhibiting severe sado-masochistic traits, many terrible enactments marked those ten years. These enactments were much worse during the weekends, indicating his great vulnerability to separations. Often on Monday, I would find myself worried for his safety. But analysis worked as it should, as it sometimes does. His symptoms resolved and he stopped the dangerous, self -destructive behaviors he had engaged in. He changed careers from a sterile job in finance to a creative field where he began to experience moderate success. Though not in love, he maintained a relationship that had warmth and tenderness with a young woman.

So, we projected a date for termination (terrible word, I fear!) for a year ahead.

Two weeks before that date, during a Friday session, at 7AM, and in the last few minutes of the session, Betto exclaimed, while laughing with glee, "Oh, I guess you may not have listened to the news. An Argentine pilot confessed to having thrown victims of kidnapping and torture, alive, into the River Plate. I can imagine those faces as they fell."

No, I had not heard the news. I absorbed this in horror.

For me, those faces had names.

I wanted to but could not respond for several minutes. When I did, I just said, "Those are powerful images, perhaps we may hold onto them until next week, to try to understand their meanings."

A college student knowing only basic psychoanalytic ideas could probably produce an interpretation: "Facing the end of your 7-year analysis you feel thrown out into the sea." A college student who was not Argentine born, or who did not feel she had miraculously escaped the fate of those victims.

So, when I spoke, I could barely articulate some fragment of secondary-process thinking, but I could not really absorb the complex meaning of his communication.

What I said earlier about the vulnerability of the exile to the onslaught of memories that have been carefully repressed is evident here. Like Celeste, I had tried to keep myself isolated from terrible painful images that events could mobilize without warning.

I also suspect that a less-vulnerable clinician might have revised the date of the end of that analysis. But I did not. And only later did I think that leaving him out into the sea was my punishment to him for the brutality of the experience he had subjected me to. I was exiling him.

Fortunately for Betto – and for my psychoanalytic conscience! – he did return a year and a half later for a brief but immensely productive few months. Then, only then, could we address that moment of that dramatic Friday session in all of its important meanings, including obviously the depth of his fury at me for letting him go.

Final Reflections

At the time these pages are being edited, the world is going through a more terrible situation than we have ever lived. Exile is more dramatic in the context of this tragic moment, but so is every painful situation we can imagine.

Does my conjecture about this phenomenon, the exile of memories, have any relevance? Any clinical relevance? Any technical implications?

In the context of my clear awareness of Freud's (1912) epigram about the impossibility of destroying someone "in absentia or in effigy," what can we, Freudian analysts, offer?

As psychoanalysts, when working with exiles or immigrants in situations where return is impossible, forbidden, or uncertain, perhaps we may be aware of how vulnerable the patient may be to processes that are not apparent, or easily detectable.

Should we then, perhaps, consider being less "pure" in our psychoanalytic technique?

Perhaps analysis is not possible for victims of violence who are also exiles.

Should we be "educational"?

Only supportive?

Should we use a directive technique?

I am convinced that our analytic minds are essential to our own understanding and that without that understanding we cannot be helpful. These considerations, incidentally, may be particularly meaningful as we contemplate the world that opens before us in the wake of the pandemic.

Finally, a word about children. What about them? What about the specificity of the situation of being witness to or victims of violence, and never exiled by their own will?

There are concepts, such as *the moral third*, that offer a specifically useful approach (Bragin, 2019). It is possible then that treatments that are more focused, and specifically focused on the concept of trauma, will become more useful.

And yet, I want to emphasize once again that only a psychoanalytic approach allows us to reach the depth of understanding that is both essential for our patients and for our own psychic equilibrium.

References

Akhtar, S. (1999). The Immigrant, the Exile and the Experience of Nostalgia. *Journal of Applied Psychoanalytic Studies* 4:2.

Akhtar, S. (2004). *Immigration and Identity Turmoil, Treatment, and Transformation.* Lanham: Rowman & Littlefield Publ.

Amati Mehler, J., Argentieri, S. and Canestri, J. (1993). *The Babel of the Unconscious: Mother Tongue and Foreign Languages in the Psychoanalytic Dimension.* Madison, CT: International Universities Press, Inc.

Bragin, Martha. (2019). Pour a Libation for Us: Restoring the Sense of a Moral Universe to Children Affected by Violence. *Journal of Infant Child and Adolescent Psychotherapy* 18(3).

Freud, S. (1912). The Dynamics of Transference. *Standard Edition* 12:99–108.

Grinberg, L., Grinberg, R., and Festinger, N. (1989). *Psychoanalytic Perspectives on Migration and Exile.* New Haven: Yale University Press.

Harlem, A. (2010). Exile as a Dissociative State. When a Self Is Lost in Transit. *Psychoanalytic Psychology* 27(4):460–474.

Hollander, N. (1998). Exile, Paradoxes of Loss and Creativity. *British Journal of Psychotherapy* 15:2.

Nunca Más. Informe de la Comisión Nacional sobre la desaparición de personas (Eudeba, Argentina, 1984).

Szekacs-Weisz, J., and Ward, I. (2004). *Lost Childhood and the Language of Exile.* London: Imago East West.

Chapter 9

Working within the Frontiers

The IPA as a Protective Link

Rogelio A. Sosnik

I will start by recounting our fresh history.

In 2017, Stefano Bolognini, then the president of the I.P.A., presented his and other members' idea to create a committee to the board, now called Psychoanalyst Emigration and Relocation Committee (PERC), to research and better understand the challenges that psychoanalysts and candidates were facing when emigrating from their former homes to new countries.

The idea was first to study the legal conditions our colleagues needed to meet in order to reestablish their practices and then to examine the opportunities available for their reintegration into a psychoanalytic society belonging to the I.P.A.

Bolognini's idea was born from his realization that the emigration and relocation of our membership was now a much more frequent experience than had been earlier.

However, we know the psychoanalytic movement historically has a diasporic quality, mainly as a consequence of wars.

Freud and his family migrated to London; Lowenstein, Kris, Hartmann, Franz Alexander, and Annie Reich to the U.S.A.

Other migrations had to do with opportunities for new developments,

So it was for Melanie Klein, Hanna Segal, and Herbert Rosenfeld, who migrated to London.

In the present time, migration is a consequence of many dramatic events.

The United Nations reported that in 2018, 75 million people around the world were displaced from their homes by natural disasters, political, religious, and economic reasons. These waves of emigration are what have been created by the new social realities.

The migrants are facing opposition and resistance in the new desired places. Such resistance materializes in the building of detention camps, the

DOI: 10.4324/9781003266228-13

erection of walls, and the separation of family members. This also creates a new kind of internal war within the hosting countries. Pope Francis has often referred to this during his homilies.

Obviously, our colleagues are no exception to those social conditions. They share the situation of violence and economic hardship with the rest of the population.

All of this clearly justified the creation of our committee.

We started our work during the IPA presidency of Stefano Bolognini, then, under Virginia Ungar – our first female president – who strongly supported it. We continue working today as our current president, Harriet Wolfe, is a dedicated and strong supporter.

In the beginning, we requested that each society send us the names of their members and candidates who were trained in their institutes and later emigrated to other countries, and also the names of those who were trained elsewhere and later emigrated and joined their institutes and society. In the same communication to societies, the committee also requested information regarding the society's or institute's rules and regulations for applications from migrating members and candidates who would like to join their institutions. The committee started to receive important information from some of the societies, but many others did not reply at all to the request.

Almost all of the societies that responded reported not having any rules or policies about the incorporation of I.P.A. members trained outside their institutes.

It is then obvious that such a situation makes the I.P.A. appear as a removed body rather than an effective umbrella organization that can protect and effectively take care of its membership in moments of real social change.

With that in mind, we started our work with the goal to include a new level of commitment to and protection of our membership.

In 2018, we developed a "Questionnaire for I.P.A. Emigrant Members and Candidates," which was sent out to all I.P.A. members.

The committee received 177 completed questionnaires. We began to study the data in the beginning of July 2019, before the London Congress.

The call for completed questionnaires is an ongoing task, and the committee will be continually compiling this growing database for emigrant psychoanalysts.

Our concern is that we need to help and facilitate our membership to continue their relationship with our association and their sense of belonging to it. That sense of belonging is part of their identity.

During the London Congress we held a meeting with colleagues who were starting the process of leaving their countries or just trying to relocate in the countries that they moved to.

Our meeting, attended by 38 émigré members and candidates, had a strongly emotional atmosphere, where the sense of helplessness and hopelessness dominated the exchanges. The need for data about the requirements of the countries that members had moved to or were planning to move to, and the conditions to legally practice, were the predominant concern. Such concerns created a sense of proximity for all of us that was real and deeply felt.

All the members of our committee are émigré themselves. That creates a strong sense of kinship and resonance in the nature of our endeavor.

We are all psychoanalysts who went through the process of relocation in different times and with different historical circumstances from the ones that our colleagues are facing nowadays. That means that our experiences are far from identical. There are, of course, many similarities with the current situation, but our experiences are not easily transmittable. We continue building our sense of identity within the countries that we inhabit now.

We know very clearly that it is not our task to regulate or impose on the societies and institutes that compose the I.P.A. any new rules of acceptance for foreign members. We expect instead that our presence will make more conscious the need to create some new internal rules within their bylaws. The aim would be to consider this new reality: the status of the Other, our foreign colleague.

In our committee it is very clear that our task is to follow and facilitate the processes that our colleagues are following by providing all the information that we can collect and acting as a link during the time of their processes of change.

By understanding the internal processes at stake in the moment of moving and relocating, we are trying to become more effective in our task.

In this regard, as a member of PERC, I find the work of Janine Puget extremely useful.

Janine Puget, a Franco-Argentinian psychoanalyst, lived and worked in social situations of extreme violence, living in Argentina during the "Dirty

War." Such experience compelled her to reflect on the effects of social violence, both on her patients and on herself. Practicing psychoanalysis in conditions of social violence became her "reality."

Her sense of living in an "overlapping world" (1982) with her patients led her to include that social reality within the psychoanalytic frame. Here, the exploration of the role of social reality – not "the Real" of Lacanian theory – took its place within the psychoanalytic frame.

How should it be included within the psychoanalytic canon? Her question was, is it possible to include the effect of social reality without betraying the analytic stance? That started her research. She wrote many articles on the psychic effect of social violence. She elaborated further with her views on the way the psychic apparatus is structured, developing new ideas departing from the classical metapsychology.

I believe her work greatly helps to expand the understanding of the psychic work that the émigré faces when arriving at the new place.

She states that subjectivity is built from two temporal sources: one, the old and historical one, and the other, the present one. This concept helps us understand more clearly and in-depth the processes created by the experience of migration and relocation.

Her views are expanded in her article "The Subjectivity of Certainty and the Subjectivity of Uncertainty"(2010):

> I have also discussed new form of suffering that stem from conditions imposed by the social context, in this case, the expulsion from one's territory. I choose this phenomenon because of the importance that I attach both to the feelings of social belonging and to the subject's need to create stable places in a world in constant flux.

After expressing her dissatisfaction with what she considers "cracks in our theoretical models," she posits a hypothesis that accounts for the constitution of social, familial, and individual subjectivity.

She identifies the sense of belonging as part of subjectivity, coming from being with the other, in a space in between, where the concept of the unforeseeable that is tied to uncertainty takes great significance.

She states:

> Being a subject of one's own internal world and being the subject of a relationship entails different socialization paths. In the first case,

socialization results from the unfolding of the infantile world. In the second, socialization hinges on the encounter between two or more subjects, and cannot be referred to the world of childhood. Relationships between two or more subjects stem from what I call the "effect of presence". This effect produces "presentations", which have no precedent in the infantile world. Subjects' relationships with themselves, within their internal world, by contrast, belong in the "representational" world; the world we traditionally know best, which has a past that supports the present.

She continues:

What I call "presentations", (Puget, 1999) is inscribed on the basis of the effect of presence -the clash between two otherness-, which gives rise to new subjectivities. Psychoanalysis has mainly dealt with representations and object relations, and therefore with the illusory attempt to recover something that has been lost (repressed). It has aimed to give new shape to those past situations that block our present and can be conceived of as traumatic. The logic of the psychic world, which has been unfolding and exploring in great depth since Freud, and the logic of the relational (linkage) world do not coincide. I even think of them as heterologous.

Two worlds are thus confronted. One owes its formation and complexity to the setting into motion of mechanisms that depend on identification (in its various modes), as Freud and his followers have described. I call this the identity world, the world of the One, capital O. This is the world of representations and object relations, of the drive and its manifestations.

The other world, which I call the world of the Two, is founded mainly on the work demanded by the subject's exposure to the effects of otherness and foreignness in the relational world. Suffering is produced by the constant alteration of singularity, thence the idea that each link and each group creates their own subjects. And the unforeseeable as a principle takes the lead in It. In the link and in the group is the place that these subjects become alive. At the same time, we must be capable of inhabiting spaces that are ready to welcome us. This require us to do something together and transform what had been previously established into something current.

I took Puget's ideas on the constitution of the two levels that compose our subjectivity as tools to understand the mourning process and the incorporation processes that take place during the elaboration of the emigration and relocation in another country.

I start from the level of representations, the level of the One, according to Puget. Then I connect that with the situation of the societies that follow the I.P.A.

As I said earlier, almost all of the societies reported not having any rules about the incorporation of I.P.A. members trained outside their institutes. This does not necessarily mean an attitude of rejection, but a sort of denial of the diasporic reality of the psychoanalytic movement around the world. And, for the migrating member, it is a wall that they have to traverse.

With regard to the component societies of the I.P.A., it seems clear to me what their reasons are for attempting to keep their internal cultures and to preserve their own sense of identity.

The pluralistic theoretical and clinical approaches in current psychoanalysis generate in each society an environment that in some ways resemble a family that creates its own language and habits, which provide and justify to their members a sense of belonging.

Beyond the unfinished transference neurosis, more mature links exist within their members. And this situation creates new conditions that impinge upon the internal situations of the members that are changing places. They start a new process of leaving behind the "families" into which they grew.

To focus specifically on the members that are migrating, I would refer to their sense of loss. Utilizing Puget's ideas, I would describe two levels of loss.

In the first level, the one of "representation" and historical development, the experience of parting creates the sense and phantasy of becoming an orphan and an outcast who is looking for a new family to be adopted by (Oedipal structure).

In the second level, the loss of the other, the support of the sense of belonging creates the sense of becoming an alien to oneself. The feeling of depersonalization refers to the experience of being in a new culture and having to learn the rules of the new society. Often that will include the learning and use of a new language, not just the local language of the new country, but also the new "psychoanalytic language" that the new "family "shares. Such experience adds a sense of loss of aspects of the migrant's own subjectivity that depends on the fact of "to do with another."

For Puget, these two levels are heterogenous and contemporaneous: one connected with the past, the other with the present, and both are implied in the "identity crises" that conforms the process of migration and relocation.

After these considerations, and focusing on the place of the migrating colleagues, I invite you to think about the fact that beyond the common experience of migration, the relocation in the new different psychoanalytic societies implies for them a need to recover and expand their sense of identity. What the societies can offer is the possibility to be open to the task of "doing together." That provides to the newcomer the chance to recover a space to rebuild and reorganize their new places as subjects while learning the new and internal psychoanalytic language that is developing in their host society. In that regard, it is not a mystery why the attendance at discussions of clinical and theoretical papers that many societies offer to them open a window onto the current language of psychoanalysis and provides a space for them. Such a space allows them to rebuild their subjectivity and possibly start to recover their identity as psychoanalysts.

But this is not all. Our task is also to try to work with the component societies on the possibility of incorporating the newcomers as full members. In this regard, we offer the chance to work with them on the particularities that each society establishes for their full membership while also supporting the migrating members.

It is our task, then, to help our members by connecting them with the places where they relocate, with information and psychological help, acting as a presence to preserve the lost links, and, in that way, to soothe their sense of deidentification while trying to reestablish the continuity of their new lives.

References

Puget, J. (1982) "Analista y paciente en mundos superpuestos" (Analyst and patient in overlapping worlds) *Psicoanalisis* 4:503–522.

Puget, J. (2010). The Subjectivity of Certainty and the Subjectivity of Uncertainty. *Psychoanalytic Dialogues* 20(1). Routledge.

Chapter 10

Reframing Early Interventions for Refugee Populations

The Importance of Emergency Medicine in Early Detection and Delivery of Mental Healthcare

Kendall A. Pfeffer, Julia Superka, David Srivastava, and Adam D. Brown

Introduction

An increasing number of refugee (i.e., a person who is unable or unwilling to return to their country of origin owing to a well-founded fear of persecution, [UN General Assembly, 1951]) children and families have involuntarily migrated to countries around the world to seek safety and refuge in recent decades (Pieloch, McCullough, and Marks, 2016). According to a 2018 United Nations report, the number of persons displaced by conflict and disaster worldwide reached a record high of 68.5 million in 2017 (UNHCR, 2018). This includes 25.4 million refugees, over half of whom are children (UNHCR, 2018). Consequently, the number of refugees seeking resettlement exceeds current systems' capacity.

In 2016, only 189,000 refugees were resettled, and the rest remain in limbo. The number of asylum seekers awaiting refugee status has also spiked dramatically (UNHCR, 2018). As a result, many refugees and asylum seekers spend years, even decades, in unstable and insecure locations such as refugee camps or "underground" as urban refugees where resources are scarce, basic needs may go unmet, and future prospects remain precarious. Fully 85% of refugees reside in low-to-middle income countries (LMIC) (UNHCR, 2018) where mental health services are under-resourced, and 80% of those in need do not receive appropriate services (Nickerson et al., 2017; WHO, 2010). Additionally, refugees residing in high-income host countries is also a major global health priority, and one which is dependent on capacity building within existing systems of care (Abubakar et al., 2018; Nickerson et al., 2017; WHO, 2017, 2018). More specifically,

DOI: 10.4324/9781003266228-14

a recent report by WHO (2018) on mental health promotion with refugees and migrants highlights the scarcity of evidence for prevention and early treatment of mental disorders with this population and identifies promising practice principles to guide further research and development in this area. This chapter synthesizes findings pertaining to mental health care research and practice with refugee populations and proposes a framework for scalable early intervention with refugees building on the ecological systems perspective of refugee distress. We then illustrate how an immersive summer program and partnership with the Department of Emergency Medicine, University of Bern-Insel in Bern contributed to a framework in which emergency medicine becomes a critical context for early mental health detection and interventions for refugee communities.

Mental Health Risk in Refugees

Refugees are, most often, trauma survivors who flee their countries of origin due to war, political violence, famine, disease, or systemic persecution often involving torture, imprisonment, the death of family members, or other human rights violations (Steel et al., 2009; USA for UNHCR, 2018). The traumatic events they face prior to displacement are frequently prolonged, repeated, and, as is often the case with persecution, interpersonal in nature – all of which are factors associated exacerbated posttraumatic stress and depression symptoms (Nickerson et al., 2017). In addition, refugees are exposed to potentially traumatic events and physical safety risks during their migration journeys and then subsequently to a broad range of post-migration stressors in their new host countries ([see Figure 10.1]). In a three-year, follow-up study with severely traumatized refugees and asylum seekers, 62% of participants reported experiencing negative life events post-migration (Schick et al., 2018). A broad range of socio-cultural and economic post-migration stressors, commonly referred to as post-migration living difficulties (PMLD), are consistently associated with adverse mental health outcomes over and above the effects of past trauma (Das, 2018; Li, Liddell, and Nickerson, 2016; Miller and Rasmussen, 2010; Morina et al., 2018; Schick, Zumwald et al., 2016; Schick, Morina et al., 2018).

Given these traumatic stressors, PMLDs, and other challenges associated with forced migration, a diverse range of mental health concerns are commonly observed in refugee adults and children. Recent studies have

I. PRE-MIGRATION

Exposure to violence
Community violence
Forced combat
torture
War
Witnessing the death of
loved ones

Persecution
Death of family members
Imprisonment
Torture
Violation of human rights

Economic hardship
Famine
Extreme poverty
Lack of basic needs
loss of property

Displacement

II. MIGRATION

**Life-threatening events
& ongoing rights
violations**
Extortion
Human trafficking
Physical injury
Sexual violence

Travel conditions
Unsafe boats or tight,
enclosed vehicle
infectious disease
Limited access to food or
clean water

Psychological injury
Separation from family
and support systems
Survivor's guilt
Separation grief

III. POST-MIGRATION

Resettlement

Temporary
asylum

**Unstable, insecure
locations**
Dense, urban areas
Refugee camps
Temporary housing

**Chronic stress
exposure**
Basic need satisfaction
Family separation
Limited access to
resources (e.g.,
education, healthcare)
Socioeconomic factors

Acculturative stress
Discrimination
Linguistic barriers
Low healthcare and
mental healthcare literacy
Social isolation.

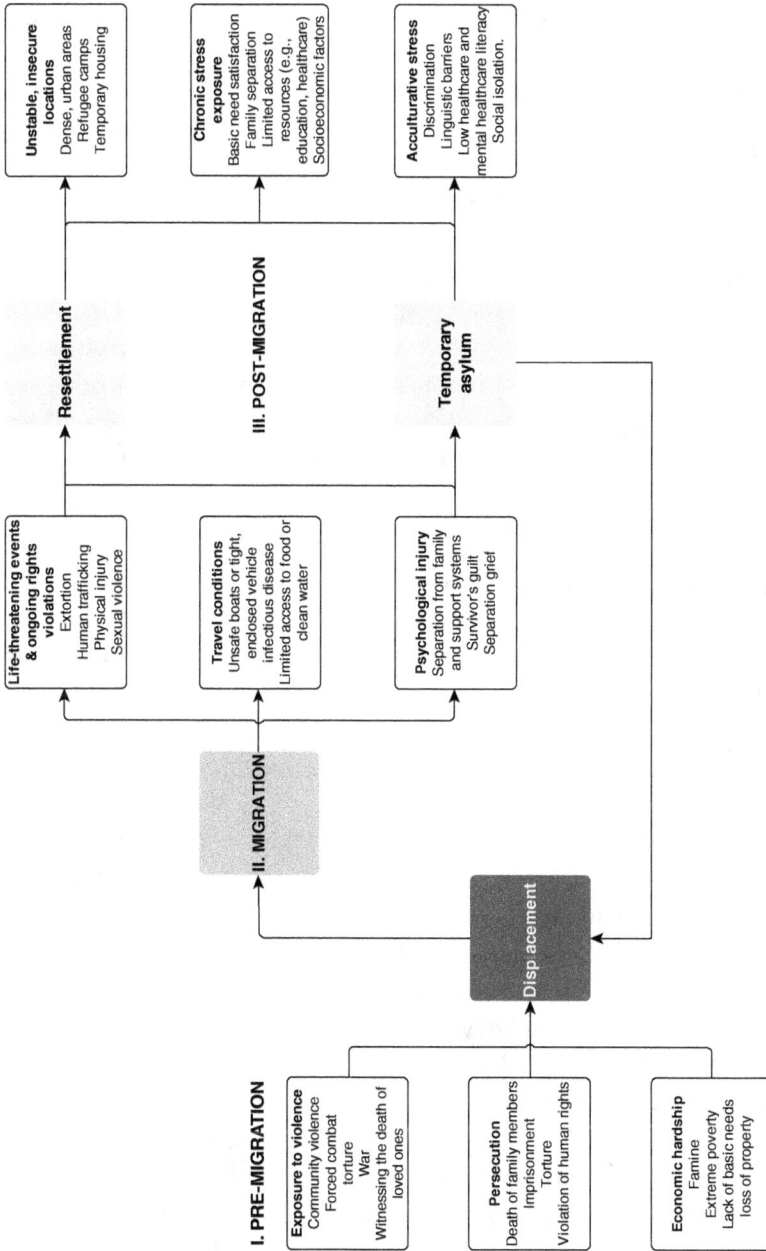

Figure 10.1 Outline of refugee trajectory, inclusive of trauma and stress exposure, risk factors and possible points of intervention

found disproportionately high rates of posttraumatic stress disorder (PTSD) when compared to host populations, as well as higher rates of depression and anxiety disorders in absolute terms (Fazel, Wheeler, and Danesh, 2005; Morina, Akhtar, Barth, and Schnyder, 2018). Increased prevalence rates of mental disorders, as well as behavioral issues and attachment problems, are also observed in children and unaccompanied refugee minors (URM) (Betancourt et al., 2012; Vervliet, Lammertyn, Broekaert, and Derluyn, 2014). Associations between somatic equivalents of distress and trauma exposure have been identified (Moisander and Edston, 2003; Olsen, Montgomery, Bøjholm, and Foldspang, 2007; Rohlof, Knipscheer, and Kleber, 2014); however, few studies have assessed rates of somatization disorders despite high rates of somatic complaints. Other post-traumatic stress reactions, such as survivor's guilt and separation grief (Hussain and Bhushan, 2009; Nickerson et al., 2014), and comorbidity, particularly among PTSD and depression, are frequent (Fazel, Wheeler, and Danesh, 2005) and suggestive of levels of clinical severity that place refugees at risk of functional impairment and disability. As such, there is an urgent need to develop effective transdiagnostic interventions and to expand the research focus with refugees from trauma-focused interventions aimed at PTSD symptom reduction to the investigation of post-traumatic psychological distress more broadly (Nickerson et al., 2017).

Early Interventions and Treatment Models

Silove, Ventevogel, and Rees (2017) highlight the theory-practice divide between accepted social ecological frameworks and the current research landscape. Ecological models of refugees' experience, such as the ecological model of refugee distress (Miller and Rasmussen, 2010) and the Adaptation and Development After Persecution and Trauma (ADAPT) model (Silove, 2013), argue the importance of developing interventions that extend beyond the narrow focus of individualized, trauma-focused approaches; however, the majority of controlled trials with refugees continue to focus on the efficacy of symptom-focused, and specifically trauma-focused, interventions.

Research examining early interventions with refugees is even more limited. Psychological first aid (PFA) represents the most common form of early intervention for recently traumatized people post-disaster and following humanitarian crises within the disaster mental health literature (WHO, 2015). Despite large-scale implementation of PFA, the authors found no randomized controlled trials examining the effects of PFA, likely due to the difficulty of conducting research in the immediate aftermath of large-scale disasters and humanitarian crises. Currently, PFA remains an "evidence-informed approach" to early intervention rather than an "evidence-based intervention" (Shultz and Forbes, 2014). As such, there is limited empirical evidence regarding the effect of PFA on targeted outcomes, such as connection to services, alleviation of acute distress, reduction in the occurrences of PTSD, or improvement in psychosocial functioning. In fact, the vast majority of the early interventions reviewed by ISTSS's Guidelines Committee for the 2018 report fall under the category of "insufficient evidence to recommend" or "emerging evidence" (ISTSS Guidelines Committee, 2018). Only CBT-T, cognitive therapy, and EMDR received the standard recommendation, none of which have been extensively evaluated with refugee populations.

Emerging Evidence: Brief, Scalable Interventions

It is worth noting that much of the research currently being conducted in early and/or brief, scalable interventions for refugees has been funded and organized by the World Health Organization (WHO) as part of a concerted effort to develop and evaluate low-intensity psychological interventions (Dawson and Rahman, 2018) that can address both the needs of refugees and dilemmas relating to feasibility, scalability, and other barriers to care inherent to intervention work with displaced populations. For instance, task-shifting is recommended by WHO to reduce the economic cost of treatment delivery and to enhance scalability and sustainability of programming in under-resourced settings. The Inter-Agency Standing Committee (IASC) guidelines on mental health and psychosocial support services (MIIPSS) also emphasize the importance of integrated and multilayered systems of support aligned with stepped and collaborative care models.

Redefining Early

Early interventions, sometimes referred to as secondary prevention, for PTSD are typically implemented within a short duration of the occurrence of a traumatic event (i.e., peri-trauma or early post-trauma period) and aim to alleviate traumatic stress reactions that may lead to chronic PTSD (Kearns, Ressler, Zatzick, and Rothbaum, 2012; Linares et al., 2017). Early interventions also generally target secondary prevention of negative sequelae and the early treatment of posttraumatic stress symptoms commonly associated with acute stress disorder (Magruder, Kassam-Adams, Thoresen, and Olff, 2016). As such, early interventions must be practical for delivery in the context of adversity or early post-trauma contexts. The question of when to intervene, and how, is particularly pertinent to this population given the often transitory nature of resettlement and the psychological impact of immobility (Jordans and Tol, 2013; WHO, 2018).

A New Framework for Early Intervention

In this section, we propose a framework for early intervention with refugees (see Figure 10.2) that arose from the review of the extant evidence regarding epidemiological studies of mental health disorders and symptoms, the current landscape of research and practice, and existing evidence regarding efficacious treatments, as well as the application of the principles of prevention and early intervention (Institute of Medicine Committee on Prevention of Mental Disorders, 2014), integrated, multisectoral stepped care models (IASC, 2007; Silove, Ventevogel and Rees, 2017), and social ecological models (Miller and Rasmussen, 2017).

Many of the challenges of addressing the health care needs for the growing population of immigrants and refugees are new and unfamiliar to care providers and health care organizations. Responsibility for mental health support to refugees is shared by a network of agencies, including the United Nations High Commissioner for Refugees (UNHCR), the World Health Organization (WHO), the International Medical Corps (IMC), government and not-for-profit organizations, mainstream mental health and specialist refugee services, and volunteer organizations. The policies applied to refugees by host countries are crucial to the mental health of that population (Silove, Ventevogel, and Rees, 2017). Patients follow varied and often complex pathways into mental health care systems, including the emergency department, direct admission, and referrals from doctors or community agencies; varying assessments are carried out that provide diverse information in differing formats (WHO, 2018). Integration of services across this vast network of organizations is complex and often means those in need fall through the cracks of an already overburdened system until symptoms reach acute crisis or disability.

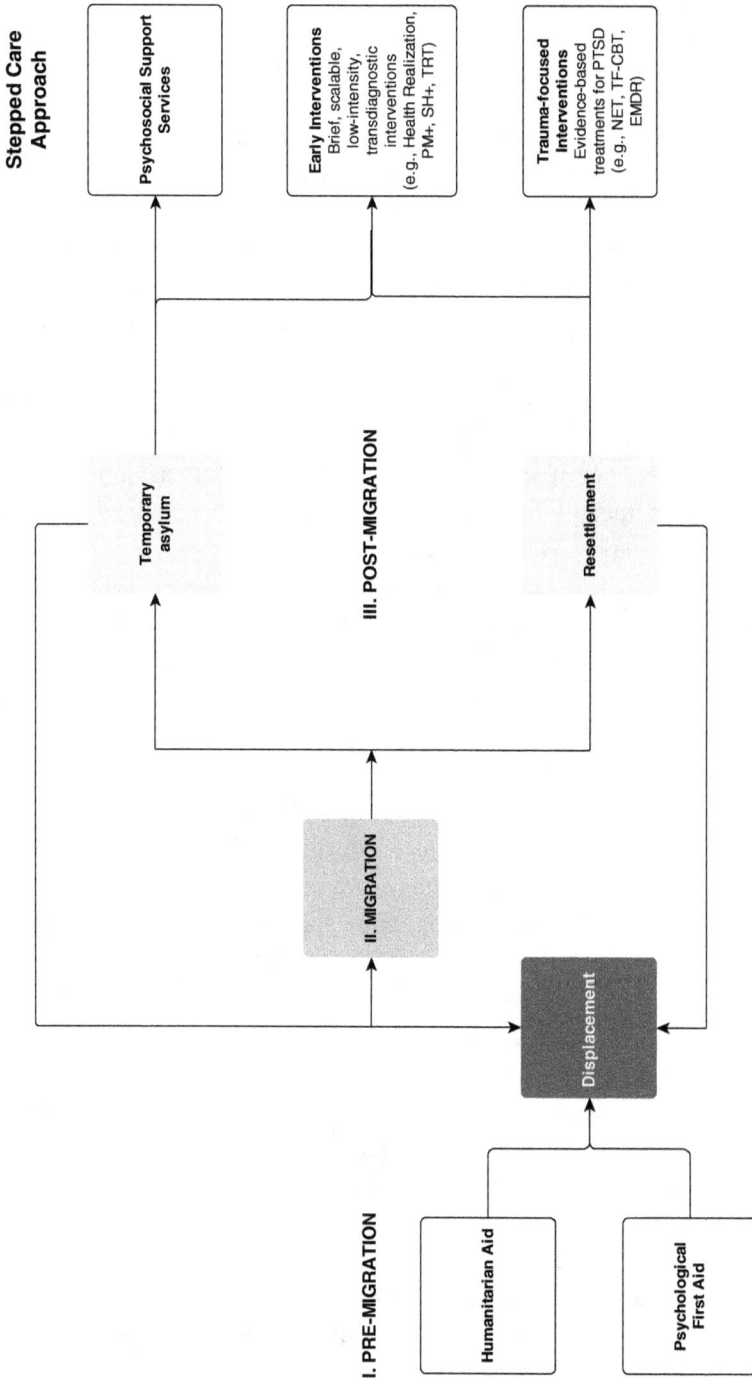

Stepped Care Approach

Psychosocial Support Services

Early Interventions
Brief, scalable, low-intensity, transdiagnostic interventions
(e.g., Health Realization, PM+, SH+, TRT)

Trauma-focused Interventions
Evidence-based treatments for PTSD
(e.g., NET, TF-CBT, EMDR)

Temporary asylum

III. POST-MIGRATION

Resettlement

II. MIGRATION

Displacement

I. PRE-MIGRATION

Humanitarian Aid

Psychological First Aid

Figure 10.2 An ecological systems framework for mental health service delivery with refugees, inclusive of feasible time points and locations for intervention

Case Study: Department of Emergency Medicine, University of Bern-Insel

Following the increase in migration from the Middle East and Northern Africa to Western Europe, Müller and colleagues in the Department of Emergency Medicine, University of Bern, carried out a systematic review of medical chart records from 2012–2016. The records revealed a steep increase in the number of emergency department (ED) visits among patients seeking asylum. In fact, patients with asylum-seeking status increased by 45 percent during this period. The patients were primarily from Somalia, Eritria, and Syria. Many of the individuals seeking care in the ED were referred to psychiatry and although a majority of the patients stated they were in "urgent need of a consultation," the average triage level did not suggest the patients were experiencing an acute medical condition.

The growing number of admissions among patients with asylum-seeking status in need of mental healthcare led to the creation of the ED Management and Migration Medicine Research and Treatment Group, led by Dr. Srivastava. In partnership with the Swiss Hospitals for Equity, they began looking more deeply into the use of the ED to more rapidly identify, refer, and deliver interventions for patients seeking asylum who might be experiencing mental health concerns.

Among the strategies being undertaken in the ED to better characterize and identify mental health issues among asylum seekers is a study using digital tablets in which patients who are not in need of acute attention are asked to complete a short survey about their well-being. The surveys have been translated into multiple languages and translation services have been made available. These questionnaires are part of a strategy to build capacity around mental healthcare within the ED through more mental health screening and to help better identify the range of symptoms and complaints expressed among patients from a wide range of cultural backgrounds. Klingberg and colleagues found that asylum seekers often pursue care in the ED rather than seeing a general practitioner, which makes this context an important first point of contact for many refugees, which, in turn, underscores the importance of developing robust mental health systems in EDs.

Building on this work, in 2019, a summer "signature project" of the Consortium on Forced Migration, Displacement and Education, launched a four-week immersive study abroad program for undergraduate students with the goal of introducing students with interdisciplinary backgrounds to a wide range of complex issues associated with forced migration in general and to engage in early intervention research in the ED in particular. For four weeks, students participated in daily didactics on the subject of displacement and mental health, shadowed physicians and researchers in the ED, and were asked to carry out independent research leading to a research proposal by the end of the four-week program.

The undergraduate students, from Vassar, Bard, and Sarah Lawrence Colleges, were immediately supervised by two graduate students (MP [Suffolk University] and JS [New School for Social Research]) and a clinical psychology professor (AB, New School for Social Research). The students were primarily asked to develop a proposal that would help provide more effective detection and early intervention for patients with asylum-seeking status and to reduce wait times and other barriers of care for such patients in need of mental healthcare. The students employed several methods for developing their proposals. First, they carried out an in-depth and extensive desk review of peer-reviewed research on mental health risks and care for refugee populations, with a specific focus on Europe. Second, the students shadowed physicians in the ED as they interviewed patients in the ED for non-acute issues who possessed asylum-seeking status. Third, the students conducted site visits and interviewed practitioners and experts from a number of relevant sectors, including WHO, UNHCR, and representatives from asylum centers.

Over the course of this research, the students began to develop a more nuanced understanding of the opportunities and challenges that exist within the various contexts they were exploring. They also engaged in sophisticated comparative analyses, in which they considered how frameworks and approaches used to support community-based, task-sharing, and peer-to-peer models of care more prevalent in other country might be adapted to Bern, Switzerland. The learning process was iterative. After each site visit or day spent researching peer-review articles, the group would meet to discuss their experiences and how it was shaping their perspectives. Often, such discussions led to more questions than conclusions, but nevertheless deepened their engagement in their work.

Based on their in-depth learning, the students developed a highly innovative framework seeking to address both acute mental health needs with a focus on early detection and early intervention as well as the creation of a non-specialist focused, community-based practice that could potentially support more long-term forms of care. Each part of the proposal was grounded in existing research and theory as well as the interventions and first-hand observations made throughout the summer. The students' proposal not only provided an analysis of the key benefits of such programs, but also some of the barriers that would need to be overcome in order to integrate into existing practices based on what they learned during their visit. The students were then invited to the US embassy to present their findings. Each student was responsible for sharing a different aspect of the proposal and they did an effective job conveying both the significance of this public health issue and answered high-level questions from state department representatives. Taken together, they made an effective case for a more integrated system of care in which local members of the refugee community play a more direct role in working alongside doctors in the ED to help identify patients in distress and to assist with follow-up and long-term psychosocial support.

Discussion

Although there is a growing body of research on MHPSS services and related challenges and barriers to care, information on interventions designed to improve service delivery or facilitate improved pathways to better care are scarce (Abubakar et al., 2018). There have been very few systematic reviews and evaluation studies specifically examining the evidence on access to mental health care and efforts to improve access, service utilization, and engagement among refugees; however, the systematic review of Satinsky and colleagues (2019) offers a useful framework for future examination (Satinsky et al., 2019). In closing, scalability, prevention, early intervention, and community-wide engagement are of critical import. As stepped care models are being proposed and implemented in line with the IASC guidelines on MHPSS in emergency settings, a range of approaches that facilitate increased scale and capacity building, including but not limited to the development of early intervention models in EDs, should be explored and systematically examined (Ventevogel, 2018; Inter-Agency Standing Committee, 2007).

References

Abubakar, I., Aldridge, R.W., Devakumar, D., Orcutt, M., Burns, R., Barreto, M.L., . . . UCL – Lancet Commission on Migration and Health. (2018). The UCL-Lancet Commission on Migration and Health: The Health of a World on the Move. *The Lancet* 392(10164):2606–2654. https://doi.org/10.1016/S0140-6736(18)32114-7.

Betancourt, T.S., Newnham, E.A., Layne, C.M., Kim, S., Steinberg, A.M., Ellis, H., and Birman, D. (2012). Trauma history and psychopathology in war-affected refugee children referred for trauma-related mental health services in the United States. *Journal Trauma Stress* 25(6):682–690. doi:10.1002/jts.21749.

Das, B. (2018). Mental Health Trauma Treatment within the Current Mediterranean Refugee Crisis. *International Journal for the Advancement of Counselling*:1–11. https://doi.org/10.1007/s10447-018-9362-y.

Dawson, K.S., & Rahman, A. (2018). Low Intensity Interventions for Psychological Symptoms Following Mass Trauma. In N. Morina and A. Nickerson (Eds.), *Mental Health of Refugee and Conflict-Affected Populations: Theory, Research and Clinical Practice* (pp. 341–356). Cham: Springer International Publishing. https://doi.org/10.1007/978-3-319-97046-2_17.

Fazel, M., Wheeler, J., and Danesh, J. (2005). Prevalence of Serious Mental Disorder in 7000 Refugees Resettled in Western Countries: A Systematic Review. *The Lancet* 365(9467):1309–1314. https://doi.org/10.1016/S0140-6736(05)61027-6.

Hussain, D., and Bhushan, Braj. (2009). Development and Validation of the Refugee Trauma Experience Inventory. *Psychological Trauma Theory Research Practice and Policy* 1(2):107–117. doi:10.1037/a0016120.

Institute of Medicine (US) Committee on Prevention of Mental Disorders. (2014). *Reducing Risks for Mental Disorders: Frontiers for Preventive Intervention Research.* (P.J. Mrazek & R.J. Haggerty, Eds.). Washington, DC: National Academies Press. https://doi.org/10.17226/2139.

Inter-Agency Standing Committee. (2007). *IASC Guidelines on Mental Health and Psychological Support in Emergency Settings.* www.who.int/mental_health/emergencies/guidelines_iasc_mental_health_psychosocial_june_2007.pdf.

ISTSS Guidelines Committee. (2018). Posttraumatic Stress Disorder Prevention and Treatment Guidelines: Methodology and Recommendations. www.istss.org/getattachment/Treating-Trauma/New-ISTSS-Prevention-and-Treatment-Guidelines/ISTSS_PreventionTreatmentGuidelines_FNL.pdf.aspx.

Jordans, M.J.D., and Tol, W.A. (2013). Mental Health in Humanitarian Settings: Shifting Focus to Care Systems. *International Health* 5(1):9–10. https://doi.org/10.1093/inthealth/ihs005.

Kearns, M.C., Ressler, K.J., Zatzick, D., and Rothbaum, B.O. (2012). Early Interventions for PTSD: A Review. *Depression and Anxiety* 29(10):833–842. http://dx.doi.org.libproxy.newschool.edu/10.1002/da.21997.

Li, S.S., Liddell, B.J., and Nickerson, A. (2016). The Relationship Between Post-Migration Stress and Psychological Disorders in Refugees and Asylum Seekers. *Current Psychiatry Reports* 18:82. doi:10.1007/s11920-016-0723-0.

Linares, I.M.P., Corchs, F.D.F., Chagas, M.H.N., Zuardi, A.W., Martin-Santos, R., and Crippa, J.A.S. (2017). Early Interventions for the Prevention of PTSD in Adults: A Systematic Literature Review. *Revista De Psiquiatria Clínica* 44(1):23–29. http://dx.doi.org.libproxy.newschool.edu/10.1590/0101-60830000000109.

Magruder, Kathryn M., Nancy Kassam-Adams, Siri Thoresen, and Miranda Olff. (2016). Prevention and Public Health Approaches to Trauma and Traumatic Stress: A Rationale and a Call to Action. *European Journal of Psychotraumatology* 7 (March):29715.

Miller, K.E., and Rasmussen, A. (2010). War Exposure, Daily Stressors, and Mental Health in Conflict and Post-Conflict Settings: Bridging the Divide Between Trauma-Focused and Psychosocial Frameworks. *Social Science & Medicine* 70(1):–16. https://doi.org/10.1016/j.socscimed.2009.09.029.

Miller, K.E., and Rasmussen, A. (2017). The Mental Health of Civilians Displaced by Armed Conflict: An Ecological Model of Refugee Distress. *Epidemiology and Psychiatric Sciences* 26(2):129–138. https://doi.org/10.1017/S2045796016000172.

Moisander, P.A., & Edston, E. (2003). Torture and its Sequel – A Comparison between Victims from Six Countries. *Forensic Science International* 137 (2–3):133–140. www.ncbi.nlm.nih.gov/pubmed/14609648.

Morina, N., Akhtar, A., Barth, J., and Schnyder, U. (2018). Psychiatric Disorders in Refugees and Internally Displaced Persons After Forced Displacement: A Systematic Review. *Frontiers in Psychiatry* 9:433. doi:10.3389/fpsyt.2018.00433.

Morina, N., Kuenburg, A., Schnyder, U., Bryant, R.A., Nickerson, A., and Schick, M. (2018). The Association of Post-traumatic and Postmigration Stress with Pain and Other Somatic Symptoms: An Explorative Analysis in Traumatized Refugees and Asylum Seekers. *Pain Medicine* 19(1):50–59. https://doi.org/10.1093/pm/pnx005

Nickerson, A., Liddell, B., Asnaani, A., Carlsson, J., Fazel, M., Knaevelsrud, C., Morina, N., Neuner, F., Newnham, E., and Rasmussen, A. (2017). *ISTSS – Briefing Paper: Trauma and Mental Health in Forcibly Displaced Populations.* International Society for Traumatic Stress. www.istss.org/education-research/trauma-and-mental-health-in-forcibly-displaced-pop.aspx.

Nickerson, A., Liddell, B.J., Maccallum, F., Steel, Z., Silove, D., & Bryant, R.A. (2014). Posttraumatic Stress Disorder and Prolonged Grief in Refugees Exposed to Trauma and Loss. *BMC Psychiatry* 14:11. http://dx.doi.org.libproxy.newschool.edu/10.1186/1471-244X-14-106.

Olsen, D.R., Montgomery, E., Bøjholm, S., and Foldspang, A. (2007). Prevalence of Pain in the Head, Back and Feet in Refugees Previously Exposed to Torture: A Ten-Year Follow-Up Study. *Disability and Rehabilitation* 29(2):163–171. https://doi.org/10.1080/09638280600747645.

Pieloch, K., Mccullough, M.B., and Marks, A.K. (2016). Resilience of Children with Refugee Statuses: A Research Review. *Canadian Psychology* 57(4):330–339.

Rohlof, H., Knipscheer, J.W., & Kleber, R. (2014). Somatization in Refugees: A Review. *Social Psychiatry* 49(11). doi:10.1007/s00127-014-0877-1.

Satinsky, E., Fuhr, D.C., Woodward, A., Sondorp, E., and Roberts, B. (in press). Mental Health Care Utilisation and Access among Refugees and Asylum Seekers in Europe: A Systematic Review. *Health Policy.* https://doi.org/10.1016/j.healthpol.2019.02.007.

Schick, M., Morina, N., Mistridis, P., Schnyder, U., Bryant, R., and Nickerson, A. (2018). Changes in Post-migration Living Difficulties Predict Treatment Outcome in Traumatized Refugees. *Frontiers in Psychiatry* 9:476. doi:10.3389/fpsyt.2018.00476.

Schick, M., Zumwald, A., Knopfli, B., Nickerson, A., Bryant, R.A., Schnyder, U., . . . Morina, N. (2016). Challenging Future, Challenging Past: The Relationship of Social Integration and Psychological Impairment in Traumatized Refugees. *European Journal of Psychotraumatology* 7. doi:10.3402/ejpt.v7.28057.

Shultz, J.M., and Forbes, D. (2014). Psychological First Aid. *Disaster Health* 2(10):3–12. doi:10.4161/dish.26006.

Silove, D. (2013). The ADAPT Model: A Conceptual Framework for Mental Health and Psychosocial Programming in Post Conflict Settings. *Intervention.* https://journals.lww.com/interventionjnl/fulltext/2013/11000/The_ADAPT_model___a_conceptual_framework_for.2.aspx.

Silove, D., Ventevogel, P., and Rees, S. (2017). The Contemporary Refugee Crisis: An Overview of Mental Health Challenges. *World Psychiatry* 16(2):130–139. doi:[10.1002/wps.20438].

Steel, Z., Chey, T., Silove, D., Marnane, C., Bryant, R.A., and van Ommeren, M. (2009). Association of Torture and Other Potentially Traumatic Events With Mental Health Outcomes among Populations Exposed to Mass Conflict and Displacement: A Systematic Review and Meta-analysis. *JAMA* 302(5):537–49. doi:10.1001/jama.2009.1132.

United Nations General Assembly. (1951). Convention Relating to the Status of Refugees. *United Nations, Treaty Series* (189):137. www.refworld.org/docid/3be01b964.html.

United Nations High Commissioner for Human Rights (UNHCR). (2018). Global Trends: Forced Displacement in 2017. www.unhcr.org/5b27be547.pdf.

USA for UNHCR. (2018). What is a Refugee? www.unrefugees.org/refugee-facts/what-is-a-refugee/.

Ventevogel, P. (2018). Interventions for Mental Health and Psychosocial Support in Complex Humanitarian Emergencies: Moving Towards Consensus in Policy and Action? Theory, Research and Clinical Practice. In *Mental Health of Refugee and Conflict-Affected Populations.* https://doi.org/10.1007/978-3-319-97046-2_8.

Vervliet, M., Lammertyn, J., Broekaert, E., Derluyn, I. (2014). Longitudinal Follow-Up of the Mental Health of Unaccompanied Refugee Minors. *European Child and Adolescent Psychiatry* 23(5):337–46. doi:10.1007/s00787-013-0463-1.

World Health Organization (WHO). (2018). *Mental Health Promotion and Mental Health Care in Refugees and Migrants (Technical Guidance on Refugee and Migrant Health).* Copenhagen: WHO Regional Office for Europe.

World Health Organization (WHO). (2017). *Promoting the Health of Refugees and Migrants – Draft Framework of Priorities and Guiding Principles to Promote the Health of Refugees and Migrants.* Geneva, Switzerland: World Health Organization. World Health Assembly, A70/24, Provisional Agenda Item 13.7.

World Health Organization and United Nations High Commissioner for Refugees. (2015). *mhGAP Humanitarian Intervention Guie (mhGAP-HIG): Clinical Management of Mental, Neurological and Substance Use Conditions in Humanitarian Emergencies.* Geneva: WHO.

World Health Organization (WHO). (2010). *mhGAP Intervention Guide for Mental, Neurological and Substance Use Disorders in Non-Specialized Health Settings.* Geneva: WHO.

Index

lesbianism 115
Levenson, Edgar A. 102
Lewin, Bertram 10–11, 17, 40–41
Lewis, Aron 1
Lewisburg Federal Penitentiary 32
liberal: assumptions 104, 109; atmosphere
    67, 111, 114; fathers 60, 64; tradition
    104, 109, 119
liberalism: classical 107, 114; history of
    107, 110, 114; influence of 65, 104–105,
    107; militant 111
Lindsey, Vachel 112
Lippmann, Walter 116
literary magazines 28
Loewenstein, Rudolph 13
loneliness 21, 52
Lorand, Sandor 37, 48, 50
loss: of self 133, 138, 149; separation and
    17–18, 77, 97, 100, 138
Lowenfeld, Henry 13
Lunbeck, Eizabeth 108

Machiavelli, Niccolò di Bernardo
    dei 108
Mack Brunswick, Ruth 10, 79–80
Macpherson, C.B. 108–109
Mahler, Margaret 13, 16, 37, 48
Malkin, Jocelyn 84
Manent, Pierre 108
Manning DJ 109
Marcuse, Herbert 115
marginalization 107
Marxist 43, 48, 105, 107, 109, 114,
    119, 125
mass psychology: assumptions 114, 117;
    evolution of 4, 103–105, 108–109
McCarran, Pat 33–34
McCarthy, Joseph 26–29, 31, 35
McCarthyism, Age of 26
McCormick, Thomas 116
melancholy 2
memory/memories 5, 78, 96, 124, 133,
    137, 140
Menninger Clinic 48
Menninger, Karl 48
mental disorders 152, 154, 156
mental health: literature 154; professional
    60; services 151–152, 156–158, 160
mental health and psychosocial support
    services (MHPSS) guidelines 155, 160
Mesmerism 109
Meszaros, Judith 3

migration: forced 2, 126–127, 152, 159
    (see also émigré); prewar 3; process of 150
militant liberalism 111
Mitchell, Stephen 99
moderates 30–31
moral support 64, 67–68, 113
morality 116
mothers 57, 59–60, 75
mourning process 50–51, 100, 138–140, 148
movements 1–2, 104, 114, 118–119,
    127, 139
Müller, Jan-Werner (et al 2016) 158
multilingualism 134
Mussolini 81, 106, 112

narcissism, primary 115, 117–118, 125
narcissistic 77, 97, 105–106, 118
National Socialism 101
Nazi: movement 112, 124; persecution 51,
    57, 82, 98; proponent 65–66; scourge
    101–102; threat 76
neo-liberalism 108, 114–115
Neubauer, Peter 15–16
Neuer, Alexander 72
Neuer, Bettina 68
Neuer, Ruth 72
New Deal 28, 107, 111–113, 116
New Freedom 111
New Women 59–60, 75
New York Psychoanalytic Society (NYPS)
    10, 12–13
New York University (NYU) 1
NGO (non-governmental organization) 54
North America 3–5
nostalgia 133–134, 137–138
Nuremberg Laws 38

obstacles 10, 14
oral history 60
organization: American 45; anti-fascist
    28; collective 112, 114, 136; labor 110;
    nationalistic 66; paramilitary 136; small
    12; underground 27; volunteer 156
orgone boxes 32
Ornstein, Paul and Anna 53, 96
overlapping world 147

Palü, Piz 62
panic 12
parallels 121, 124–125
paramilitary organizations 136
paranoia 38, 114

For Product Safety Concerns and Information please contact our EU
representative GPSR@taylorandfrancis.com
Taylor & Francis Verlag GmbH, Kaufingerstraße 24, 80331 München, Germany